HAVE WE BECOME A SELF-DEFEATING COMPLACENT SOCIETY?

IT'S THE ECONOMY, STUPID!

A quick evaluation of the US economy reveals why Donald J. Trump was elected president in spite of eight years of continuous recovery since the financial collapse of 2008!

CHRISTOS A.

PAGE PUBLISHING, INC.
New York, NY

First originally published by Page Publishing, Inc. 2018

ISBN 978-1-64214-390-4 (Paperback)
ISBN 978-1-64214-391-1 (Digital)

Printed in the United States of America

Contents

From The Author   5

Introduction   9
   Democratic Capitalism   9
   Corporatism   10
   Social-Market Capitalism   10
   The Pros and Cons of Capitalism   11

PART 1: The Current State of Affairs
   The US Economy   15
   The Military Industrial Complex   23
   Automation, Software, and Digital Technologies   26
   Offshoring Jobs   29
   The Minimum Wage and Corporate Lobbying   31
   Worker Unions   38

PART 2: Balancing the Budget
   Higher Minimum Wage Does Not Kill Job Growth   45
   The Enormous Defense Budget   51
   Health Care, Welfare, and the Homeless   55
   Welfare for the Rich   63
   War on Drugs   69

PART 3: Making a Difference
   Making America Great Again   77

Conclusion   95

Bibliography   105

Chart and Graph Credits   127

From The Author

First and foremost, I must say that I do not consider myself an "expert" on the economy but more of a serial entrepreneur with opinions about economics, finance, and public policy. I am a professional business owner (as a general contractor, my company renovates large multifamily communities in the southeast US), I am an avid researcher (I genuinely love research work), and I am the occasional author. In the last six years, I have written and published three books, all admittedly passion projects of mine.

My first book, CYPRUS: The Island of Aphrodite, published in 2011, is a travel guide dedicated to the Greek island of Cyprus. My second book, UCHRONIA?: Atlantis Revealed, published in 2014, touches on several controversial topics and mysteries of our past. In 2017, New York City Big Book Awards voted UCHRONIA?: Atlantis Revealed as one of their Distinguished Favorites!

As my last two books imply, it is no secret that like most people, I love traveling, and I find amusing the occasional mystery that can stimulate one's imagination. On a more somber note, though, as in the case of many fellow Americans, I am deeply concerned with the current economic and public policies shaping our country today, which is the real reason behind my latest undertaking.

I started my research on this book in the spring of 2016 and finalized it a few months after the presidential election. During a very heated political year and an exceedingly divided country, I wanted to better understand voter sentiment toward the presidential candidates, the federal government, and the US economy.

Since the market collapse of 2008, I felt that the growing economy which helped the housing market, the banking institutions, and Wall Street recover, did not carry everyone else along with it as it should. Indeed, as I discovered, stagnating and poverty wages, not only in the last ten years but for the past four decades, led to the current crisis where today more than 100 million Americans rely on some form of government assistance. Millions more are barely surviving with income just above the poverty threshold, and let's not ignore that there are nearly three million homeless people in this country, many of them families with children, the fastest-growing segment of the homeless population.

This apparent failure of both the system and the politicians to look out for the well-being of every American, especially those in the lower and lower-middle class, left millions of people feeling neglected. This neglect, which in the last twenty years turned into resentment toward Washington, was more evident during the last election than in any other election in modern times.

My objective was to find the data on this public sentiment and statistically illustrate why political catchphrases like "Real Change" or "Make America Great Again" deeply resonated among frustrated Americans on both sides of the aisle, much deeper than election pollsters and the media had expected. I also wanted to demonstrate that the longing behind the political slogan to "Make America Great Again" in the eyes of most Americans did not necessarily connect the country to some distant tainted past, as some in the media suggested, but for tens of millions of distraught Americans, it meant reviving the American Dream, a dream of a land where life is better, richer, and fuller for everyone.[1]

This book is intended to familiarize the average individual with the fundamentals of the US economy, to help them better understand the essential choices politicians currently make on their behalf, and to allow them to demand better alternatives for themselves and their families.

---

[1] *The American Dream as defined by James Truslow Adams in 1931 in his book The Epic of America.*

A government of the people,
by the people, and for the people
shall not perish from the earth.

—Abraham Lincoln, 1863

Capitalism is defined as an economic system characterized by private or corporate ownership of capital goods, by investments that are determined by private decision, and by prices, production, and the distribution of goods that are determined mainly by competition in a free market.

—Merriam-Webster Dictionary

Introduction

The history of capitalism can be traced back to the early forms of merchant capitalism, which was established in the late sixteenth century in Western Europe. Traders in London and Amsterdam were the very first to creatte joint-stock companies, and from that, the first stock exchanges and banking institutions were founded. In the last five centuries that followed, merchant capitalism evolved into various other types. The following three forms are prime examples of capitalist economies.

Democratic Capitalism

It is a political, economic and social ideology that combines a democratic political system, with a capitalistic economic system. It is based on a private-sector-driven economy, which itself is based on a democratic policy, economic incentives through free markets, and fiscal responsibility. In contrast to corporatism (another form of capitalism), this type of capitalism is controlled by a democratic system that is ruled by the majority. The phrase "We the people, for the people, by the people" leaves little doubt, at least in the mind of Abraham Lincoln, that the United States as an economic system was fashioned after this form of capitalism.

Interestingly, though, while democratic capitalism stands in contrast to corporatism, the profound corporate lobbying on the American government by special interests in the last thirty to forty years seems to have shifted the power from the people and placed it in the hands of major corporations (see "Corporatism").

Corporatism

Corporatism, or corporatocracy, is the sociopolitical organization of society by major special interest groups with affiliations to various businesses in the private sector. This laissez-faire type of capitalism (a policy of letting things take their own course without interfering), which ultimately favors corporations and places them over the needs of people, is an economic system in which transactions between private parties are free from government intervention, such as regulation and tariffs.

A word of caution, though. As innocent as this economic system may appear on the surface, one must not ignore Senator Ron Paul's dire warning that America is "slipping into a fascist system where it's a combination of government, big business and authoritarian rule, and the suppression of the individual rights of each and every American citizen."

In 2012, at a rally speech given in Kansas City, the former Texas Republican (then a presidential candidate) compared the US economic model with that of Mussolini's Italy of the 1920s to the 1940s, during a time when Italy's economic corporatism had similar control over the government. Interestingly, on that very topic, Benito Mussolini quoted something similar. He said, "Fascism should more appropriately be called corporatism because it is the merger of state and corporate power."

Social-Market Capitalism

In this form of capitalism, also known as a social-market economy, industry and commerce operate by private enterprise within limits set by the government to ensure equality of opportunity, plus social and environmental responsibility.

A social-market economy, which combines private enterprise with regulations and state intervention to establish a fair competition, generally goes against the policies of corporatism, the publicly regulated economies of socialism, and the state-dominated capitalism, another form of capitalism carried out today by China and modern-day Russia.

Social-market capitalism is primarily used in Western Europe and Japan.

The Pros and Cons of Capitalism

As with any ideology and economic system, there are certain benefits and disadvantages with capitalism. The following is a list of advantages and disadvantages:

Advantages:

- It creates opportunity. While people work entirely for their financial prosperity, to increase their wealth, they often start new businesses. This job creation by the private sector ultimately helps others. The products and services these businesses also produce further improve life in the community.
- Capitalism can provide an equal opportunity for anyone who is willing to work and become financially independent.
- It is a more efficient economic system. In contrast with other economies, capitalism produces goods that are more in demand while competition creates incentives to cut costs and avoid waste.
- It promotes economic growth. Increased market wealth often leads to higher living standards for all.

Disadvantages:

- Social benefits can be ignored. Without regulations to assure a balance between the needs of business and people, corporations often tend to focus entirely on profits, and in the process, they can ignore people's needs. By nature, corporations are set up not to be concerned about people's needs, such as health care, education, personal financial stability, or a comfortable retirement. Their focus is their bottom line, and their loyalty rests with their investors, not the general public.

- Free capitalism ignores externalities. A company often overlooks negative externalities, such as pollution during production, a practice that undoubtedly destroys the environment and ultimately harms life.
- Capitalism can lead to a monopoly power. Unregulated capitalism enables companies to ultimately gain monopoly power in product and labor markets. The companies with monopoly power can easily exploit their position and charge higher prices for their goods or services.
- Monopsony exploitation happens when unemployment turns out to be too high or too many people compete for the same position. This situation often enables companies to exploit workers by setting lower wages and often employ fewer workers than during a competitive market. Also, in an unregulated system, like that of the US, every economic crisis can become an opportunity for a company to lower wages. Moreover, the continuous influx of cheap foreign labor into the country, who are willing to work for the minimum wage, is another way for corporations to force the local workforce to compete for the same low pay.
- It can lessen the need for manpower. Increased competition leads to ways of increasing production via mechanical means. This leads to automation, and as a result, many people lose their jobs to machines.

PART 1
The Current State of Affairs

The US Economy

To many people around the world, the name United States is synonymous with wealth and prosperity. Millions of people from Europe to Asia, from Russia to the Middle East, imagine Americans living in plush houses, driving bigger-than-life cars, and comfortably raising their families in stress-free environments. They believe wages and work benefits in the US are some of the best in the world, not to mention the belief that Americans are provided with the best education and health care on the planet. In short, the United States is still viewed as the land of opportunity and a place where people can effortlessly raise a family and make their dreams come true.

Little do they know, though, that both health care and higher education cost more in the United States than in any other country, and the standard of living in the place that once was called the land of milk and honey is fast disintegrating.

Truth be told, the quality of life in the US over the last forty years degraded so much; the American Dream (a dream of a land where life is better, richer, and fuller for everyone, a place where children grow up to earn more than their parents) for most Americans is now nothing but a distant fantasy. Many Americans will attest to the fact that making ends meet is becoming harder and harder year after year.

Indeed, due to the stagnating wages in the last four decades, today (according to the Census Bureau), one out of every three

Americans, more than 100 million, cannot sustain themselves without some form of government assistance. Even worse, more than 3.5 million people in the US experience homelessness each year. Of the homeless population, 35 percent are families with children, which now is the fastest-growing segment of the homeless population. Another 23 percent are US military veterans, and 25 percent are children under the age of eighteen. A recent report shows that one in thirty American children were homeless at some point last year. That's about 2.5 million children, and an 8 percent increase to a historic high, according to the National Center on Family Homelessness. Just over half of these kids are younger than six years old.

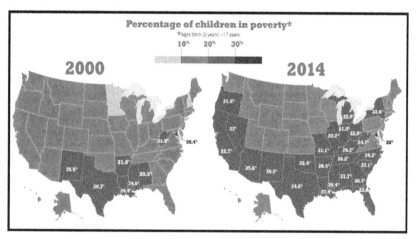

Meanwhile, while recent health-care laws (under a threat of a tax penalty) forced millions of uninsured people to buy a health-care coverage, still, more than 13 million Americans (5 percent of the US population) could not afford the cost of coverage, and they remain uninsured. Thus, they risk becoming financially ruined or even homeless in the event of a catastrophic illness.

As for the proportion of American high school graduates who go on to college (a figure that regularly rose for decades), it now appears to be declining as well. In 2014, with less disposable income and high tuition costs, only 65 percent of high school graduates enrolled in college, down from 70 percent previously.

Every day, more and more Americans realize that the America of yesterday is not the America of today. Still, even with the deficient economic conditions that currently exist, hundreds of thousands of people continue to immigrate to the United States each year, and all have high hopes for a better future for themselves and their families.

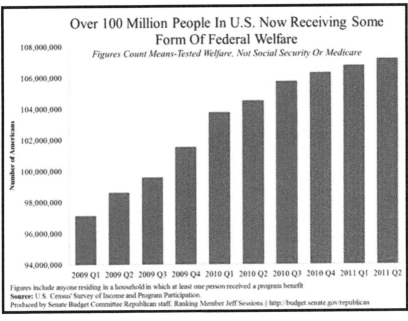

Unfortunately, though, most of the immigrants today come from less prosperous countries where ordinary wages are much lower than the minimum wage currently in America. So while this continuous migration of people into the US provides local companies with unlimited labor force eager to work for minimum wage, this influx of cheap labor into the country eventually forces the local workforce to compete for the same low wages. A survey conducted by the US Census Bureau discovered that the real median income of households supported by a foreign-born person increased by 4.3 percent between 2013 and 2014. In contrast, the median income of households maintained by a native-born person declined by 2.3 percent. And as if working for a minimum wage is not bad enough, many employers today, to keep away from offering full-time workers health-care benefits (as required by law), convert many low-income full-time positions into part-time ones, thus flooding the economy with workers who cannot sustain themselves.

To make matters even worse for US employees, American companies now have the power to manipulate the forty-hour workweek without paying overtime for more than eight hour workdays, and at any time, they can terminate one's employment without cause, without notice, and without severance pay. At-will employment is no longer considered illegal practice.

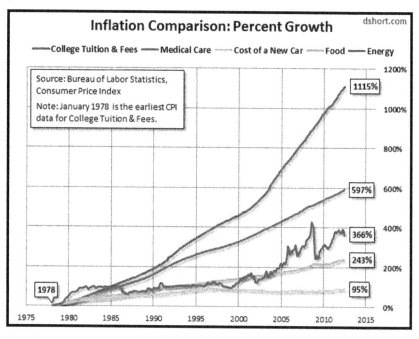

Employee rights and benefits are slowly being ignored in the interest of corporations, and essential social services, such as higher education and health care, which are offered free in many other countries, in America those are provided at a super-premium price. The heavily favored pro-corporation political system does not regulate (as in other nations) employee benefits, vacations, maternity leave, etc. Indeed, other than enforcing a forty-hour workweek and setting the minimum wage rate, nothing else is mandated by the government.

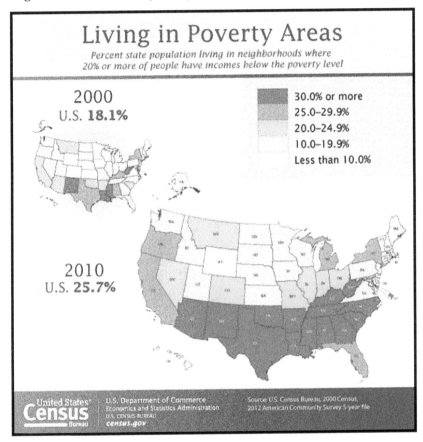

And as if this was not good enough for American employers, the US government is regularly heavily lobbied by hundreds of powerful corporations asking for even fewer regulations and more freedom in how to run their workforce. Consequently, without a proper government in place to defend employee rights and with no worker unions to push for living wages and higher employee standards, salaries and work benefits are entirely left up to the individual company. Not surprisingly, employee benefits in the US currently rank at the bottom of the scale among other industrialized nations. For example, the United States remains one of eight countries in the world where the state does not mandate paid maternity leave, and it is currently the only wealthy nation where employers are not required by law to offer employee vacation to their workers.

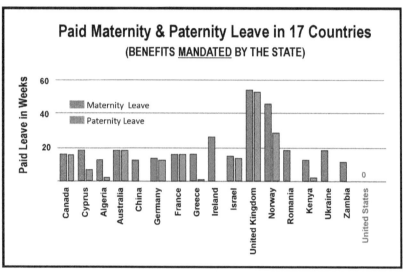

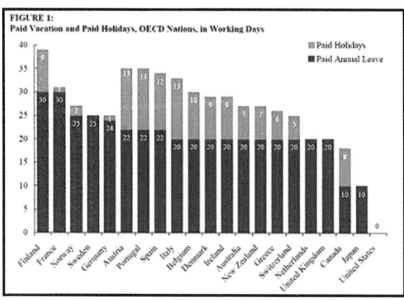

FIGURE 1:
Paid Vacation and Paid Holidays, OECD Nations, in Working Days

So what happened to the America of yesterday? How did the wealthiest nation on earth, once known for equality and opportunity for everyone, lose its affluent middle class and find itself in a situation where a large segment of the population, one out of every three of its citizens, live in poverty and, whether they are working or not, are unable to adequately provide for themselves?

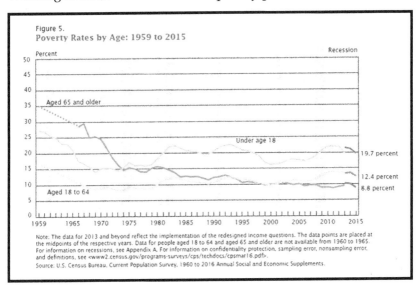

Figure 5.
Poverty Rates by Age: 1959 to 2015

Note: The data for 2013 and beyond reflect the implementation of the redesigned income questions. The data points are placed at the midpoints of the respective years. Data for people aged 18 to 64 and aged 65 and older are not available from 1960 to 1965. For information on recessions, see Appendix A. For information on confidentiality protection, sampling error, nonsampling error, and definitions, see <www2.census.gov/programs-surveys/cps/techdocs/cpsmar16.pdf>.
Source: U.S. Census Bureau, Current Population Survey, 1960 to 2016 Annual Social and Economic Supplements.

Indeed, two-thirds of all welfare recipients are employed families with income below the poverty level. According to the Census Bureau, today, out of a total population of 322 million, more than 109 million people live in households that receive federal welfare benefits. Of these people:

- 51,471,000 are food stamp recipients.
- 22,526,000 receive benefits under a women/infants and children program.
- 20,355,000 receive supplemental security income.
- 13,267,000 receive housing subsidies.
- 5,442,000 receive temporary assistance to needy families.
- 4,517,000 receive another type of assistance.

This social spending costs the United States between 668 billion and up to 1 trillion dollars annually, and ranges between 20 and 25 percent of the entire federal budget.

Of course, immigrants and native-born workers who are willing or have no choice but to work for poverty wages or even those who rely on welfare are not the reason behind America's economic woes. And while recently some politicians and the media shifted their attention and now suggest that illegal immigration is the problem, in truth, this is the least of all problems that ultimately pushed America into the current economic state. The real problems are many — they are more complex, and they go as far back as early as the 1950s.

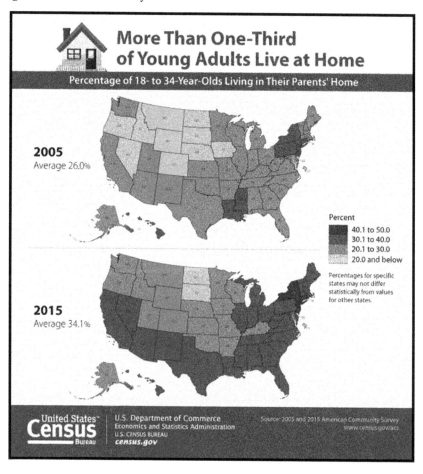

The Military Industrial Complex

During World War II and for the first time in US history, American industries had effectively converted to defense production as the crisis of the war demanded. Out of this temporary conversion to satisfy the needs of a nation at war, a permanent armaments industry of considerable size emerged. An immense and powerful industry, all new to the American experience, was officially born. This influential industry that demanded higher and higher budgets did not go unnoticed by the 34th president of the United States, Dwight D. Eisenhower, a military man himself.

In his farewell speech in 1961, Eisenhower cautioned the American public not to fail to understand the grave implications of an enormous armament and suggested to guard against the increasing power and influence the military industrial complex had over the government. He also counseled Americans to be vigilant in monitoring the military industrial complex and guard against their acquisition of unwarranted influence. He said,

"Only an alert and knowledgeable citizenry could compel the proper meshing of the huge industrial and military machinery of defense with our peaceful methods and goals so that security and liberty may prosper together."

During Eisenhower's time, the US annual military budget was less than 300 billion when adjusted for inflation. Since Eisenhower and all the way to 2001, the average annual budget was around $350 billion (see chart below). After the September 11 attacks, it gradually escalated to nearly $700 billion, while during the Afghanistan and Iraq wars, special funding pushed the annual spending over a trillion dollars. This sudden massive increase in military spending, which partially was achieved with borrowed funds, nearly crashed the American economy.

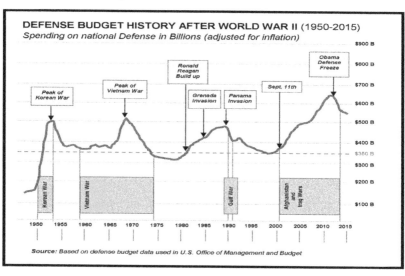

The chart above indicates the defense spending since World War II in inflation-adjusted dollars. (The above numbers do not include benefits to veterans.) There are big spikes along the way, one for the Korean War and another for the Vietnam War. During the 1980s, there was a huge increase in spending under Ronald Reagan. The additional funds were used for the invasion of Panama, Grenada, and the Gulf War. The final spike came after the attacks of 9/11. It's worth mentioning that funding for both the Iraq and Afghanistan wars was paid separately from the annual budget, and that cost is not shown in the chart above.

Currently, the United States invests more than $800 billion annually on military, military services, and its various defense departments—more than the entire budget of the next thirteen wealthiest nations combined. This annual expense, which amounts to 20 percent of the entire federal budget, has to be one of the reasons why America cannot balance its annual budget.

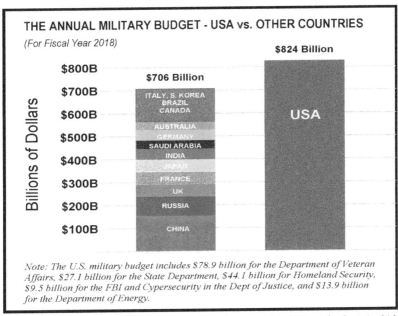

Note: The U.S. military budget includes $78.9 billion for the Department of Veteran Affairs, $27.1 billion for the State Department, $44.1 billion for Homeland Security, $9.5 billion for the FBI and Cybersecurity in the Dept of Justice, and $13.9 billion for the Department of Energy.

In comparison to the United States, China's annual military budget is $166 billion, Russia's $90 billion, and UK's $60 billion.

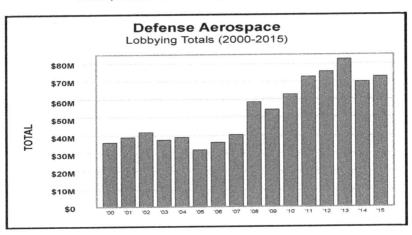

Automation, Software, and Digital Technologies

Many people born in the 1950s and 1960s still remember the fascinating promise of future technologies, such as flying cars, smart homes, and optical telecommunications. Half a century ago, automation and advances in robotics were making promises of a better, more productive future.

Today, fifty years later, most of these technologies are already in use. Although we don't quite yet own flying cars, and every household does not come with a robot, robotics today, whether we realize it or not, play a significant role in our everyday lives.

As it turned out, though, in addition to higher productivity and the ability to build and sell products for less; automation is also to blame for manufacturing jobs lost and for stagnating wages.

While automation and digital technologies are not quite recognized yet as the culprits behind millions of jobs lost, in truth, according to Harvard Business Review, between 1995 and 2002, just in a span of seven years, some 22 million manufacturing jobs were lost worldwide due to automation, while at the same time, productivity soared by 30 percent (see chart on page 27).

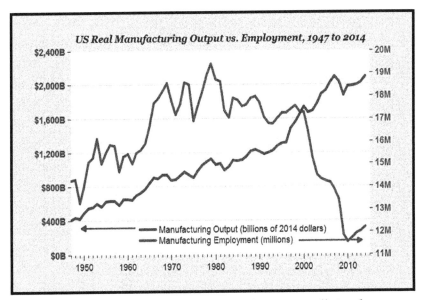

*After 2001, manufacturing employment drops at an all-time low,
while manufacturing output rises to an all-time high.*

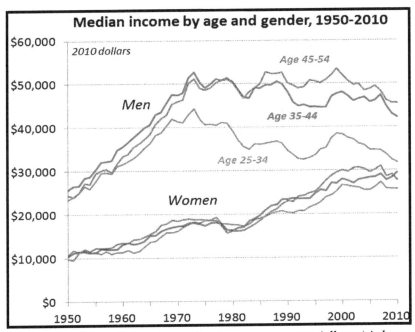

*When adjusted for inflation, the median income among men (all ages) is lower
today that the median income during the 1980s.*

Without a doubt, factory automation is behind millions of good jobs lost in America today, as it provides a substitution of machinery in place of human labor. Even more troubling is the fact that more computer-guided automation is creeping into everything, from manufacturing to decision-making, which foretells a future in which robots will reduce the need for human workers, while the remaining few jobs will require much higher skills and credentials. Indeed, most displaced people in the last twenty years had no training or the education needed to reacquire any of the remaining manufacturing jobs which required more advanced technological skills. And the manufacturing jobs continue to shrink. While in the 1980s, employment in manufacturing was 22.1 percent (two out of every ten jobs), today it is down to only 10.2 percent (one out of every ten jobs).

To make matters worse, in the last twenty years, in addition to automation, software and digital technology also displaced many types of jobs involving routine tasks, such as accounting, payroll, clerical work, and forced many of those workers to take other lower-wage positions or, depending on their age, to abandon the workforce entirely.

Automation, software, and digital technology, at least in part, are behind the low number of available manufacturing jobs and for the rising income inequality that confronts the United States and other countries in the developed world today. They are in part behind the disappearance of the middle class in America.

No longer having a choice, more and more Americans, once recipients of middle-class income, are forced to accept lower-paying jobs. Many older workers, with five years or so away from retirement, are no longer looking to replace their former well-paying jobs and either retire early and live off their retirement savings, or they are forced to work for a minimum wage job so they can hold on to a health-care coverage, which they desperately need.

Offshoring Jobs

As it appears, a significant number of jobs that were not eliminated by automation, software, and digital technologies were ultimately exported to other countries with much lower wages and primarily to China. Actually, nearly 3.5 million jobs have been outsourced to China since 2001.

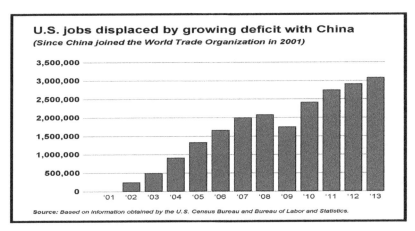

It is worth noting that this ongoing competition with low-wage workers from other less-developed countries, such as

China, ultimately determines the wages for workers in the US and reduces the bargaining power of non-college educated workers with similar skills throughout the local economy.

Undoubtedly, jobs outsourced to China and other less industrialized countries not only helped diminish employment opportunities in the US but also helped contribute to the wage erosion in America, especially since 2001, when China entered the World Trade Organization. Between 2001 and 2013, the US goods trade deficit with China increased by $240.1 billion or by $21.8 billion on average per year over that period. And over the 2001–2011 period, US workers who were directly displaced by trade with China lost a collective $37 billion in wages as a result of accepting other lower-paying jobs. Regrettably, for the US economy, this enormous disposable income is no longer around to be recaptured by the US marketplace.

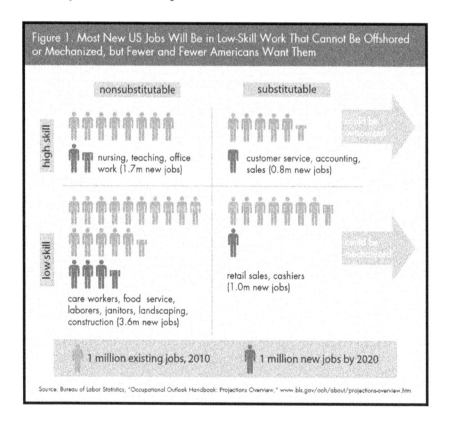

Figure 1. Most New US Jobs Will Be in Low-Skill Work That Cannot Be Offshored or Mechanized, but Fewer and Fewer Americans Want Them

Source: Bureau of Labor Statistics, "Occupational Outlook Handbook: Projections Overview," www.bls.gov/ooh/about/projections-overview.htm

The Minimum Wage and Corporate Lobbying

The general logic in the United States, especially in the past few decades, is that raising the minimum wage could be bad for the economy. This, of course, excludes the opinion of the millions of people who try to make a living while earning the minimum wage.

The belief is that higher wages will ultimately reflect on the goods produced or on the overhead of any company which in turn must raise its prices to cover the higher operating cost of production. This general logic is what corporations, politicians, and the media often use to convince the public that raising the minimum wage could be bad for the overall economy (especially during troubled times). The result of that mentality is that the minimum wage paid in 1968, at $1.60/hour, when adjusted for inflation, equaled to $10.52/hour and had $3.27/hour more buying power than that of the minimum wage today, which was recently raised to $7.25/hour. To be more clear, the annual gross income of a minimum wage recipient, before taxes, is now $15,080, while after taxes, the net income drops down to around $12,740, which borderlines the poverty threshold set by the US government at $12,331! This means a contribution to a health-care coverage program will drive the net income of the minimum wage recipient below the poverty level.

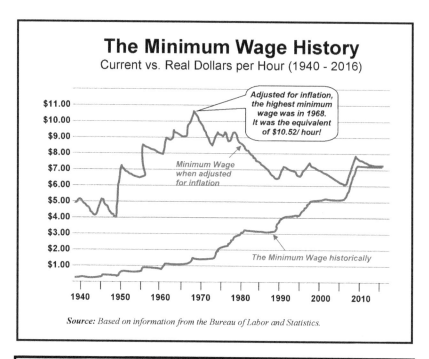

The Minimum Wage History
Current vs. Real Dollars per Hour (1940 - 2016)

Adjusted for inflation, the highest minimum wage was in 1968. It was the equivalent of $10.52/ hour!

Minimum Wage when adjusted for inflation

The Minimum Wage historically

Source: *Based on information from the Bureau of Labor and Statistics.*

Poverty Thresholds for 2015 by Family Size and Number of Related Children Under 18									
	Related children under 18 years								
Size of family unit	None	One	Two	Three	Four	Five	Six	Seven	Eight or more
One person (unrelated individual)									
Under 65 years	12,331								
65 years and over	11,367								
Two people									
Householder under 65 years	15,871	16,337							
Householder 65 years and over	14,326	16,275							
Three people	18,540	19,078	19,096						
Four people	24,447	24,847	24,036	24,120					
Five people	29,482	29,911	28,995	28,286	27,853				
Six people	33,909	34,044	33,342	32,670	31,670	31,078			
Seven people	39,017	39,260	38,421	37,835	36,745	35,473	34,077		
Eight people	43,637	44,023	43,230	42,536	41,551	40,300	38,999	38,668	
Nine people or more	52,493	52,747	52,046	51,457	50,490	49,159	47,956	47,658	45,822

Source: U.S. Census Bureau.

In 2014, the official poverty rate in America was 14.5 percent. In other words, nearly 47 million Americans lived in poverty, an increase of 2.3 percent since 2007. Interestingly, between 2013 and 2014, poverty rates went up even on people with a university degree as well as married-couple families. Worth mentioning is that nearly 44 percent of the entire US workforce currently earns less than $10 an hour!

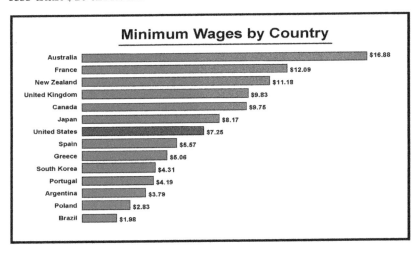

So what is happening? How can the US allow wages to remain so low that for minimum wage earners to survive, they have to enroll in some government assistance program? Can't the politicians who oppose raising the minimum wage, in fear of hurting the economy, see that the population in the US living in poverty has essentially grown exponentially to the point that social programs today at a trillion plus annually are beginning to cripple the federal budget and the country they serve?

To solve this problem, shouldn't politicians demand that private companies hire and pay employees with real living wages? Why must taxpayers obligate themselves to bail out corporations (whose sole existence is profit) and in effect assist them to become even more profitable by subsidizing their workers' wages with government assistance? In a capitalist system, should private for-profit companies have the right to expect financial bailouts from time to time or, as in this case, expect the American taxpayer to be supplementing their worker wages so they can remain profitable? If so, are these companies benefiting or milking the economic system? Even more importantly, how do they get away with such an arrangement?

The truth is, most decisions that govern America today are not made by the elected politicians but by the very corporations who insist (via lobbying) on paying their employees' wages that borderline poverty. Major corporations today, on the average, spend about $2.6 billion a year on lobbying the US government ($1.18 billion lobby the House and 860 million the Senate). Currently, the biggest private companies in the US have upwards of 100 lobbyists each representing them and allowing them to be everywhere in Washington DC!

Annual Amount Spent on Lobbying & Number of Lobbyists by Year (2000-2016)

Number of Lobbyists	Year		Total Spent
12,544	2000		$1.5 Billion
11,853	2001		$1.6 Billion
12,150	2002		$1.8 Billion
12,959	2003		$2.0 Billion
13,201	2004		$2.1 Billion
14,098	2005		$2.4 Billion
14,494	2006		$2.6 Billion
14,827	2007		$2.8 Billion
14,142	2008		$3.1 Billion
13,732	2009		$3.5 Billion
12,918	2010		$3.5 Billion
12,619	2011		$3.3 Billion
12,237	2012		$3.3 Billion
12,130	2013		$3.2 Billion
11,842	2014		$3.2 Billion
11,535	2015		$3.2 Billion
11,167	2016		$3.1 Billion

Source: Calculations are based on data from the Senate Office of Public Service

When lobbying started in the 1950s and 1960s, political representation was more balanced. Labor Unions were much more important, and public interest groups were more powerful to counter corporate lobbying. During that time, lobbying was rather clumsy and ineffective with very little ability to influence congressional votes. Things changed, though. Today business lobbying is among the most significant transformations in

American politics. Business lobbying has built itself up over time and has increasingly come to overwhelm every other potentially neutralizing force. It also changed how corporations interact with government. Rather than keeping government out of corporate business, companies now bring the government in as a partner, looking to see what their country can do for them.

Organized lobbying began in 1972 in an environment of growing compliance costs, slowing economic growth, and rising wages. Around that time, a bunch of leading CEOs formed the Business Roundtable, an organization that was devoted explicitly to cultivate political influence. Many companies during this period began to hire their first lobbyists. At first, they were able to kill a major reform law, rolled back regulations, lowered their own taxes (from the top rate of 70 percent down to 50 percent and the low rate of 14 percent down to 11 percent), and more importantly, they helped move public opinion in favor of less government intervention in the economy. By the 1980s, through organized lobbying, corporations have already accomplished everything they set out to do. Public trust in the federal government also all but disappeared (see chart below). But they did not stop there!

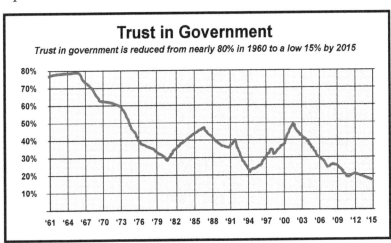

Trust in Government
Trust in government is reduced from nearly 80% in 1960 to a low 15% by 2015

Today, what makes lobbying so different from the 1970s is that major corporations now have the resources to manipulate government policy on almost any level. They no longer hope to influence government decision-making, but they help write some of the policies the government often enacts into law. For example, pharmaceutical companies, going back as far as the 1980s, opposed the idea of government bargaining power through bulk purchasing, an act that obviously would have reduced the drug industry profits. Worth noting is that through bulk purchasing is how Canada and several European nations can provide their citizens affordable prescription drugs. At the first opportunity, around the year 2000, industry lobbyists proposed and lobbied the bold idea of the prescription drug benefit, known as Medicare Part D, in essence an agreement that explicitly prohibits bulk purchasing by the US government, thus allowing the pharmaceutical companies to pocket an additional $205 billion profit over a ten-year period.

So who holds the minimum wage at the level where it is today? Obviously, the very same corporations who don't realize that poverty wages, year after year, leave less and less disposable income in the US economy for their products and services.

The latest increase in the minimum wage, at $7.25/hour, was in July of 2009, more than six years ago. Since then, it did not change, not even to match inflation, which varied each year from 1.5 percent to 3.2 percent. The take-home pay of a minimum wage recipient, at $7.25/hour, equals $245 a week (after Social Security and Medicare taxes). The net annual income, based on a forty-hour-workweek, is roughly $12,740 (or $1,062/ month), barely a few hundred dollars above the poverty threshold. Of course, in addition to contributing to health-care coverage, the minimum wage worker, with a net income of $1,062/ month, must pay for rent and other living expenses, not an easy thing to do, considering the rent for a one-bedroom apartment in the United States averages at $1,100/month. While the cheapest one-bedroom in the US is located in an Iowa zip code at $420, the price of one-bedroom in Honolulu, Hawaii, is $1,833, which explains why Hawaii's homeless population began to soar in the last few years. It also explains why in most states a recipient of $7.25/hour has no choice but to enroll for a government assistance. It seems to be the only way to survive. We must not forget that the average cost of utilities is $300/month, or that it takes $45 to fill up a car tank with gas, and that auto insurance costs an average of $100/month, not to mention money needed for food, clothing, childcare, etc.

It is worth mentioning that if the minimum wage had risen along with worker productivity and inflation since the early 1950s, today it would have been set at $21.72/hour! Still, a recent much more modest proposal to raise the minimum wage to $10.10 over a period of three years failed to pass the Congress.

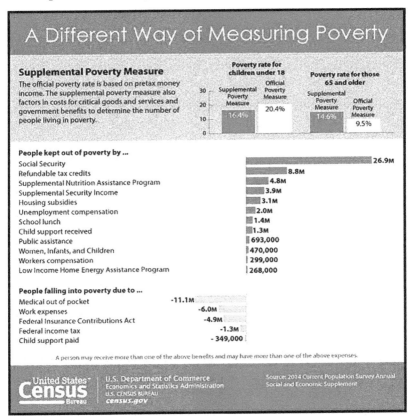

People in the US continue to fall into poverty due to medical expenses and the high cost of health care.

Worker Unions

The labor movement in America grew out of the need to protect the common interest of workers specifically in the manufacturing and industrial sector. It goes back to the late 1700s, during a period of a free-labor market. Over the years, organized labor fought for better wages, reasonable hours, safer working conditions, health-care benefits for employees, and for worker compensation to injured workers. Employee unions can also be credited for eliminating child labor in the workplace.

Politically, the founding doctrine of unionism meant an arm's-length relationship to the state and the least possible entanglement in partisan politics.

The formation of the Federal Society of Journeymen Cordwainers (shoemakers) in Philadelphia in 1794 marked the beginning of the trade union organization in America. From that time forward, craft unions defended their trades against cheap labor and increasingly demanded a shorter workday. Things did not improve overnight, though. In fact, even with union demands, it took nearly one hundred years (at around 1890) for the average seventy-plus-hour workweek to drop down to sixty hours, and then another thirty years (at around 1919) before workers won their forty-hour workweek (although that was still not official.) It also took another ten years after that before companies allowed for a five-day workweek.

In the 1960s, the labor movement's historic commitment to support primarily skilled white male workers was soon to be labeled discriminatory by more progressive labor leaders, who ultimately deployed the labor's power during John F. Kennedy's presidency.

From the 1970s forward, deregulation in the communication and transportation industries, as well as an unprecedented onslaught of foreign goods from a more globalized market, started a non-union competition. Concession bargaining between unions and factories became widespread, and plant closings decimated union memberships.

With the election of Ronald Reagan in 1980, came to power one of the most anti-union administrations since the 1920s during the Harding era. By 1985, union membership dropped by 5 million, and for the first time, the unionized labor force in America fell below 25 percent while mining and construction union memberships were totally annihilated. By the end of Reagan's presidency, only 17 percent of American workers belonged to unions, half the number of the early 1950s.

While by the end of the 1980s, worker unions, good or bad all but disappeared, during the same period organized corporate lobbying intensified. This corporate control over the US government led to the recent erosion of employee rights, such as "at-will" employment. It allowed for companies to outsource American jobs to other countries with cheaper labor force and to pay American workers some of the lowest wages in recent history. Without unions in the last forty years to counter corporate lobbying and fight for workers' rights, corporations have been able to manufacture and promote the notion that low and stagnating wages are a good thing for the US economy. In fact, while the minimum wage today, when adjusted for inflation, is lower than that of the late 1960s, through intense lobbying, corporations have been able to block every effort to raise the minimum wage and convinced the general public that higher minimum wages will ultimately increase the cost of goods and hurt the economy.

What corporations are not telling the general public, though, and what the heavily corporate controlled media is not reporting (see chart below) is that the American middle class began to disappear at the same rate as worker unions were decimated, and the minimum wage today, which drives more and more people to live in poverty, shifts the burden of responsibility from the employer and places that on the US government's shoulder (in essence the taxpayer) who in turn must support over 100 million Americans who cannot provide entirely for themselves.

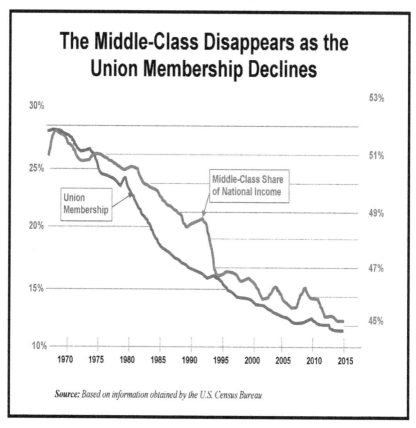

Source: Based on information obtained by the U.S. Census Bureau

As it appears, since corporations are solely motivated by higher annual profits rather than for the well-being of the economy or the country, they fail to see the bigger picture and to realize that the disappearance of the middle class, as well as the fact that one out of three Americans is left without any disposable income, will ultimately impact their bottom line.

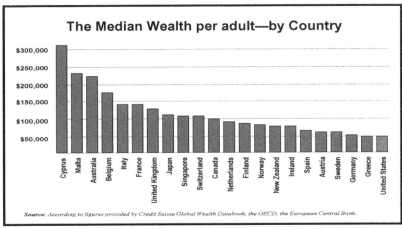

The Median Wealth per adult—by Country

Source: According to figures provided by Credit Suisse Global Wealth Databook, the OECD, the European Central Bank.

The median wealth (median net worth) per person should not be confused with the mean wealth (average net worth), which is rather misleading. For example, in the United States, the presence of several billionaires, such as Warren Buffet and Bill Gates, highly skew the numbers and drive the average net worth per person way up. (Forbes estimates that there are 540 billionaires in the United States, with a combined net worth of $2.3 trillion!) In contrast (from bottom to top along the net worth scale), the median wealth is based on the average of the more than 115 million households in the US and paints a more accurate picture. To demonstrate how vastly different the two averages can be, the mean wealth in the United States, according to Credit Suisse Global Databook (2016), was estimated at $344,692, while the median wealth (the real personal wealth) was estimated at $44,977, both vastly different numbers, not to mention disconcerting at the same time. Of course, as troubling as it is to see the median wealth of the "most prosperous" country at the bottom of the scale among other industrialized nations, even more troubling is that the median net worth in America in 1962 (when adjusted for inflation) was roughly $10,000 higher than today. And that is not all. While statistics show that by 2007 (after four decades), the personal net worth of Americans rose to an all-time high at $115,000, the economic collapse of 2008 drove the median wealth down to $65,000, where it since declined to an all-time low at $44,977! So where did all that personal wealth go? Because for most Americans, the equity in their home comprises the most significant portion of their net worth, it is not unusual to presume that the loss of median wealth after 2008 was primarily due to the housing crisis. Oddly enough, though, as the housing market and Wall Street fully recovered, the median wealth never bounced back. Instead, it is now 60 percent lower than that of 2007. Why? If anything, this demonstrates that millions of American households not only lost their home during the recent crisis but, along with it, their entire net worth, not to mention that millions more depleted their savings and 401(k) accounts. Finally, this proves that the economic recovery of the last eight years may have indeed restored the US economy and Wall Street but did not improve the lives of those hurt by the recent recession. At least not yet.

PART 2
Balancing the Budget

Higher Minimum Wage Does Not Kill Job Growth

The United States can start to restore its economy by first raising the minimum wage, thus reducing the overall number of people currently living in poverty. Of course, while raising the minimum wage will not solve all America's problems, the goal, in this case, is to reduce the number of people who currently rely on government assistance. Higher minimum living wages will not only stimulate the economy but will ultimately help the US generate substantial savings on social programs.

For the United States to achieve such an undertaking on a national level, though, especially with all the congressional opposition and intense corporate lobbying against it, would be difficult, if not impossible. Several attempts of the US government over the years to raise the minimum wage failed. The latest failure was a recent attempt to raise it at $10.10/hour.

The truth is, even if they were successful to raise the minimum wage nationwide at the intended $10.10/hour, in many states, this would not have improved the overall problem with poverty. While undeniably such a raise could have helped millions of people, especially those living in poor states, in reality, a $10/hour wage can make no difference in states with very high costs of living (not to mention that a big spike on minimum wage could hurt the job growth in the poorest states).

Unlike the traditional economies of other nations that can be managed by a single centralized government, the United States is made up of a mixture of several local governments with diverse economies, each presenting its own set of challenges. We must not ignore that the wealth as well as the cost of living in every state is different. While a worker in Iowa with apartment rent averaging $450/month would have benefited from such a raise, the same pay raise would have made no significant difference for a worker in Hawaii or Washington State where rent averages $1,800/month. Knowing this, the federal government should not be imposing on states how to run their economies but rather should provide guidelines and recommendations on how each state can improve its economy and the lives of the local work-force. Encouraging a little market competition among the states may also be more beneficial than imposing universal solutions for all. Removing certain decision-making from the political gridlock of Washington DC and truly forcing each state to determine its own minimum living wage may be the way to go. Next time the federal government attempts to raise the minimum wage, instead of trying to enact a nationwide pay raise, it may be more benefi-cial if Washington successfully promoted and sold the idea that each state, along with its annual budget establishes a minimum living wage, more suitable with its individual economy. While, for instance, the existing minimum wage at $7.25/hour may be sufficient in Mississippi, other wealthier states with much higher costs of living, such as New York, may need to adjust theirs to $10 or $15 an hour or even higher in order for workers in those states to stay afloat and out of welfare. The minimum wage for each state should be based on that state's cost of living.

States with the lowest poverty should be able to use their annual savings from social programs and divert those funds into improv-ing their local infrastructure, an investment that in itself will provide even more well-paying jobs. At the same time, a federal Fair Act should penalize states with higher-than-normal poverty rates rather than providing them with additional financial aid. Incompetency in running a state's economy should not be rewarded with additional assistance. Furthermore, social benefits by the federal government should be equally distributed based on each state's population rather than the state's ability or inability to run its economy.

If such an idea sounds reasonable, the question becomes, is it possible to convince states and local governments to adopt such a plan that will ultimately reduce poverty as it improves local markets with an influx of disposable income? Can the overall US economy be improved if the task was placed in the hands of local and state governments? The answer is an absolute *yes*! In fact, this is already happening across the United States and without the federal government's oversight.

What about the dire warning that raising the minimum wage could hurt the economy? Can higher minimum wages kill jobs? In truth, twenty-six states already, on their own, have voted and raised the minimum wage as they have realized workers could not sustain without government assistance. So what happened to the economy in those states? Did raising the minimum wage kill jobs, or did the pay increase have any adverse effect on their economy? Not really! In fact, the exact opposite happened. According to the Center for Economic Policy Research, thirteen of those states that increased their minimum wage saw higher employment growth (by an average of 0.68 percent) than those states where the minimum wage did not change.

San Francisco, for instance, a city where the minimum wage is set at $10.74/hour, the highest in the country, has seen faster job growth than any other big city over the last ten years. Likewise, Washington State, which has the highest state minimum wage in the country, at $9.47/hour, has seen faster job growth than any other state. During 2014, while Seattle's employers were absorbing the higher-paying wages, unemployment decreased 17.56 percent, falling from 6.3 to 5.2 percent.

As of January 1, 2017, the city of Seattle, which recently had the minimum wage set between $10.50 to $13/hour (depending on the size of the company and number of employees), raised its minimum wage to $15/hour. The good news is that New York and California recently also signed laws to raise their minimum wage to $15/hour. And as more and more states realize that raising the minimum wage does not have the negative impact that corporate lobbying warned us about, more are now in line to raise their minimum wage as well. And while minimum wage increases like these may not entirely fix the economy in every state or in the entire country, it is undoubtedly a step in the right direction to minimize poverty while the local markets benefit from the additional disposable income.

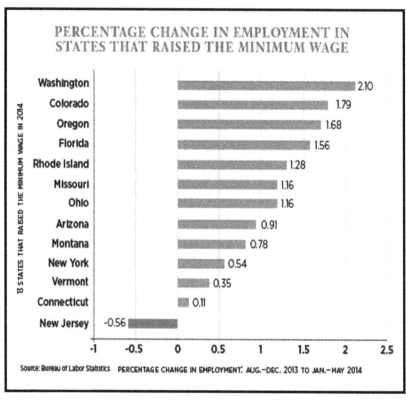

PERCENTAGE CHANGE IN EMPLOYMENT IN STATES THAT RAISED THE MINIMUM WAGE

Source: Bureau of Labor Statistics   PERCENTAGE CHANGE IN EMPLOYMENT. AUG.-DEC. 2013 TO JAN.-MAY 2014

Since 44 percent of the entire workforce in the United States works for less than $10/hour, any increase in pay over that will help improve the lives of 62 million workers. And if the minimum wage was to be raised to the anticipated $15/hour (a real living wage) that could reduce the number of people relying on government assistance by as much as 50 percent, a positive change that would ultimately help the federal government save more than $300 billion annually from various welfare programs.

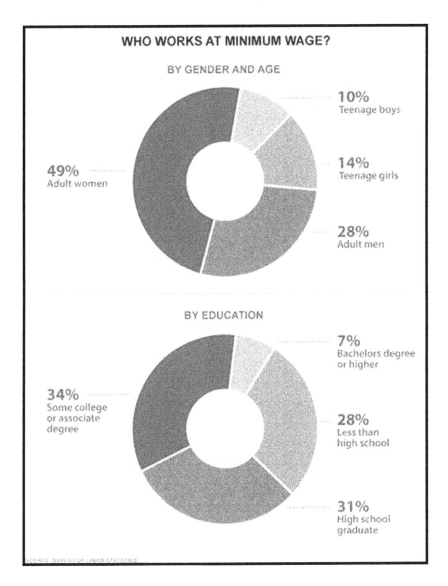

As for those who are concerned that such a pay increase would raise the cost of certain goods, such as fast food for example, indeed, that is true. A recent study revealed that if the minimum wage were to be increased from $7.25 to $15 per hour, the price of a Big Mac, for instance, would have also gone up by 17 cents (from $3.99 to $4.17), a rise of 4.3 percent. A nominal cost when considering that such a pay increase would boost the disposable income of 66 million people by half a trillion dollars annually. That's a lot of buying power for everyday goods. Walmart will never again complain that every time gas prices go up its profits plummet!

In essence, raising the minimum wage (an idea primarily supported by Democrats) has the very same result as lowering one's taxes (an idea favored by Republicans). Both concepts allow more disposable income in the hands of the consumer to help stimulate an ailing economy. The advantage of raising the minimum wage, though, rather than just lowering taxes, is that a $15/hour living wage will also help reduce the number of people on welfare by at least 50 percent and, in doing so, save the taxpayers $300 billion annually. These savings can help balance the federal budget.

The Enormous Defense Budget

While the United States, as a military superpower, should maintain its ability to solve global conflicts if and when needed, the question is, should it continue to invest in defense more than all the other wealthy nations combined? Historically, in the last fifty years, the average defense budget of the US during peace (when adjusted for inflation) ranged around 350 billion dollars. The next chart shows that during the last fifty years, the United States increased its regular defense budget three times.

The first time was between 1966 and 1972 to cover the cost of the Vietnam War. By 1975, once the war was over, the annual defense budget was reduced back to $350 billion. Later on, with the arrival of Ronald Reagan, there came another spike in defense spending that lasted between 1983 and 1994. This time, the additional funds were used for the Grenada invasion, for the Panama invasion, and finally for the Gulf War. By 1994, and after the end of the Gulf War, the military budget once again was ultimately reduced to the regular annual budget of $350 billion. For seven years, it was kept at around that level. After the September 11 attacks, the military budget was gradually increased through the roof to fight the Afghanistan and Iraq wars. For the first time in

51

US history and more than ten years consecutively, the military budget remained above 600 billion annually. When taking into consideration the overall cost of Homeland Security, Veterans Affairs, the cost of other miscellaneous defense activities, including the defense-related paid interest, the US annual budget for defense currently exceeds 1.2 trillion dollars. Can this be the new norm? If so, what will the budget be next time there is another war? How high is the US government willing to let it go?

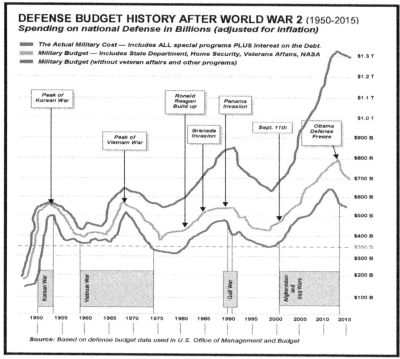

To put things in perspective, since the budget surpluses of 1998–2001, in the eight years that followed, the federal debt was raised from 6 to 12 trillion dollars primarily to cover the cost of the Afghanistan and Iraq wars (the actual cost of wars is not included in the annual federal budget). Of that, 2 trillion dollars went to medical care for wounded veterans.

After the market collapse of 2008, 1 trillion dollars more had to be "invested" to bail out the Wall Street and the banking institutions. Since then, during the recovery period of the last eight years, 5 trillion dollars more were added to the national debt, which now stands nearly at $20 trillion. Currently, the United States pays 266 billion dollars annually just to cover the interest on this enormous debt.

In other words, almost 7 percent of the entire federal budget of 3.9 trillion dollars goes toward the interest, and this is during a time when interest rates globally are low. As interest rates world-wide climb, the interest rate, as well as the annual cost to cover the interest on the US debt, will automatically rise. (It's worth noting that in contrast to the 266 billion dollars the US is currently paying to cover the interest on the national debt, it only invests $42 billion for unemployment, $60 billion in higher education, 8 billion in pollution control, and $107 billion in food and nutrition assistance.)

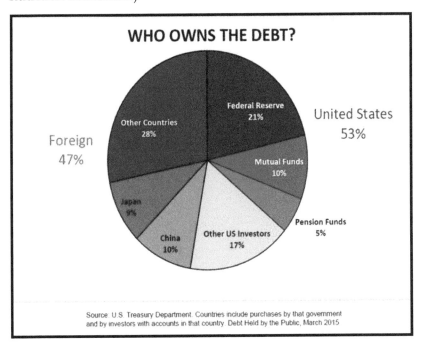

A huge portion of that interest is due to the excessive military spending. Without any major wars currently taking place, if the military budget were to return to normal, at 350 to 400 billion dollars (which still is more money than China, Russia, United Kingdom, France, and Japan spend combined), this would allow for an excess of $350 Billion annually to pay off the national debt and ultimately help balance the budget.

Health Care, Welfare, and the Homeless

There are those who claim that social programs in the United States are slowly bankrupting the country. Certainly, when considering that all social programs in the US, when combined, amount to more than 1 trillion dollars, 25 percent of the entire country's budget, this unquestionably huge number is large enough to scare anyone. When looking more closely at the overall cost, though, and especially when comparing that to what other industrialized nations pay for their social programs, this number appears to be normal. Indeed, by percentage of GDP, the US does not spend as much as several other industrialized nations. In fact, when studying the numbers a little closer, it seems that in the US, the largest portion of the expense goes to cover the high cost of health-care benefits and not to social care as many people think (see chart on page 56). As it turns out, the United States spends $9,086 per capita on health care, which is nearly double than that of other wealthy nations.

Unlike other countries where health care covers everyone, when considering that the US figure covers only those in Medicare and Medicaid, 34 percent of the population, it becomes apparent that the health-care portion of the total social spending in America is quite excessive! It is worth mentioning that employer-sponsored health care, as well as employee personal health-care expense, which amounts to an additional $600 billion, is not included in the following chart. After combining the two numbers, the actual cost of health care in the United States approaches 2 trillion dollars annually. Can Americans truly be that sick, or is it possible that America is dealing with a greedy privatized health-care system.

For the US government to begin to control the enormous expense associated with health-care benefits and health-care overall, it must start to pass new laws that would allow it to be more representative of the public, especially when it comes to the pharmaceutical industry. For example, legislation, such as Medicare Part D, should be abandoned at the first opportunity.

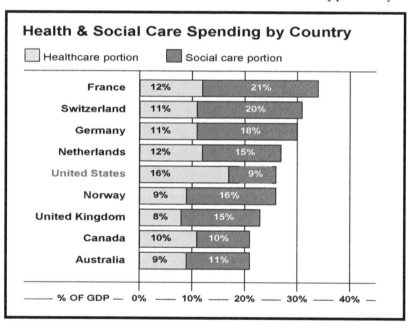

The American government, like all other governments around the world, should be able to negotiate bulk purchasing of prescription drugs with intent to sell those much cheaper to the general public. This is how Canadians can buy American brand-name drugs for pennies on the dollar. (e.g., Mirapex for Parkinson's disease costs $157 in Canada versus $263 in the

United States. Celexa for depression costs $149 in Canada versus $253 in the United States. Diovan for high blood pressure also costs $149 in Canada versus $253 in the United States. Oxazepam for insomnia costs $13 in Canada versus $70 in the US. More price examples in the chart below.)

Prescription Drugs (Monthly Cost) - By Country

DRUG NAME & COST PER MONTH	CANADA	SPAIN	UK	NETH.	USA
Celebrex (Pain)	$51	$164	$112	$112	$330
Cymbalta (Depression)	$110	$71	$46	$52	$240
Humira (Arthritis)	$1,950	1,498	$1,102	$1,498	$3,049
Copaxone (MS)	$1,400	$1,191	$862	$1,190	$3,900
Gleevec (Leukemia)	$1,141	$3,348	$2,697	$3,321	$8,500

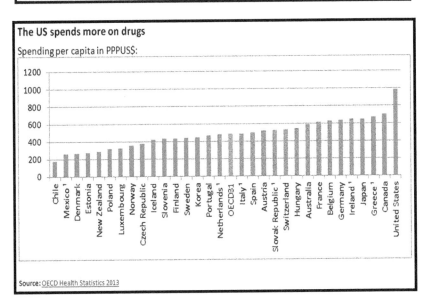

The US spends more on drugs

Spending per capita in PPPUS$:

Source: OECD Health Statistics 2013

In a capitalist society where business competition and negotiating are considered healthy practices and a monopoly is viewed as bad business, when it comes to prescription drugs, the US government should have every right to negotiate on behalf of the American people for the lowest possible prices. The same prescription drug negotiations by the federal government which could save American consumers up to $15 billion annually could also save the government an additional $6 or $7 billion on Medicare and Medicaid programs.

Another area where the federal government should step in and arbitrate is how much hospitals charge for their services and why there is a huge difference in price from one hospital to another. Most consumers today don't realize that the costs among hospitals for the very same procedure could be vastly different from hospital to hospital (even among hospitals next door to each other). For example, after viewing charges from more than 19,000 patients in the US, according to the Associated Press, a California study found that the cost for treatment of an uncomplicated appendicitis ranged from a mere $1,529 to a whopping $182,955! Why is that? How can they justify the enormous gap on this as in the case of several other medical procedures? While, of course, hospitals will say that some patients needed additional treatment or required more complicated procedures than others, the study found no cost explanation for about one-third of the cases. In other words, there is no methodology to this madness! Why are hospitals charging anything they want for their services without being held accountable? We must not forget that when a patient must visit the emergency room, carried to a hospital by an ambulance after an accident, or is urgently transported there by orders of a physician, in all those cases he or she is unaware of the treatment required and how much that service will cost at the particular hospital. There is no getting three proposals in this case before hiring a qualified professional for their services. Even when the patient is diagnosed upon emergency arrival, price negotiations are out of the question. In other words, in the case of every patient, hospitals get a blank check to fill in whatever amount they think their service is worth. No other private business in the US operates this way. No other business swindles the public as badly and in the end gets away with it. There is certainly a need for government oversight on hospital services and fees, nor only for the portion that the government pays under Medicare and Medicaid programs but also to protect the taxpayer since unreasonable hospital charges are often behind the excessive healthcare insurance premiums.

In terms of the welfare spending, it is worth pointing out that welfare costs started to get out of control since the late 1960s when the minimum wage (adjusted for inflation) was comparable to $10.52/hour. At that time, the United States was spending less than $150 billion for social programs. As the minimum wage and the buying power of the dollar declined, the segment of the population living in poverty progressively increased, and the cost of welfare began to climb.

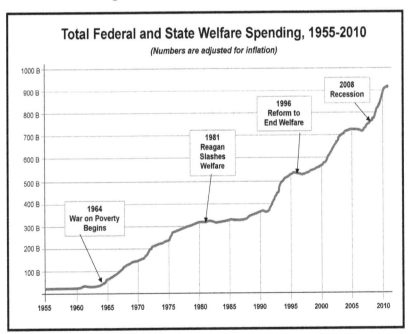

While we must take into consideration that there was a huge spike in welfare recipients immediately after the economy collapsed in 2008, it is now evident that the primary reason behind the steady increase in welfare costs is not due to one temporary crisis or another, and it is certainly not because today people are lazier than in any other decade. It is because in the past fifty years, year after year, the value of the minimum wage declined by more than $3/hour. Instead of having wages rising with the times, especially along with inflation, today, more than forty years later, 44 percent of the entire US workforce, 70 out of 160 million people, are now working for less than $10/hour – in essence, $0.52/hour less than that of the minimum wage in 1968! How can that be? How could the federal government allow this to happen?

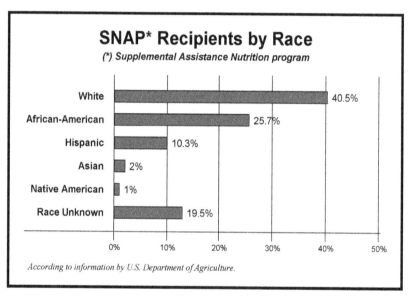

The good news is that the enormous spike in government assistance is finally noticed. Local governments finally came to the realization that the population living in poverty has grown out of control and in the last decade began to seriously affect local economies. So now that it is determined that a higher minimum wage does not have the adverse effects on the economy as we were told, half the states around the country either raised the minimum wage or are about to. Soon, with or without the federal government's involvement, the entire nation will follow, and the current minimum wage will be replaced with a living wage.

While, of course, raising the minimum wage to the recently proposed $10/hour will help only 4.6 million out of 109 million welfare recipients to leave the system, a very small number to make a significant difference to the economy, still, if 4.6 million people were taken out of the welfare system that would save taxpayers approximately $44 billion each year. And if the minimum wage were to be increased to $15/hour (a real living wage) as some states intend to do within a year or two, that will certainly cut the cost of welfare by more than half and will produce annual savings of more than $300 billion.

What about the rest of the welfare recipients, though? No matter the measures, some people will always need assistance. Let's not ignore that there will always be unemployed people, those who can get only part-time jobs, those between jobs, the disabled, or the mentally ill, who always will depend on some form of government assistance. Of course, the homeless population is of concern as well.

In terms of the homeless, every state in the US should follow Utah's example. When it comes to homelessness, most states today follow the typical approach, which is trying to make homeless people "housing ready." This common approach puts people into shelters, halfway houses, and provides them with food and medical treatment as needed until they are ready to be on their own.

Utah follows a different approach. They call their program Housing First. In 2005, there were two thousand homeless people in the state. Today they have solved their homelessness problem by offering every homeless person a home to live in. A radical idea, no doubt, but according to the director of Utah's Homeless Task Force, it is one that saved the government a lot of money. According to the Task Force, the average cost for the normal approach previously cost Salt Lake City more than $20,000 per person a year, while in comparison, putting someone into permanent housing cost the state just $8,000, which includes the cost of case managers who work with the formerly homeless to help them adjust. A Colorado study also found that the average homeless person costs the state of Colorado $43,000 a year, while housing that person would only cost them just $17,000.

Utah's Housing First pilot approach was based on seventeen individuals who were placed in homes around Salt Lake City for a two-year period, after which none of the seventeen people were back on the street. In the years since the experimental program began, the number of Utah's homeless population declined by 74 percent. The new plan not only saved the lives of nearly 1,500 people, but it saved the city $20 million annually. The overwhelming success of the experiment did not go unnoticed. More and more local and state governments are now beginning to implement the Housing First program. Considering there are more than two million homeless people in the US today, Utah's Housing First program, if implemented across the country, could save local governments more than $18 billion annually, not to mention that adding 2 million people back into the US workforce could produce another $15 billion per year in federal tax revenue. In essence, Utah's success in handling their homeless population shows that programs like Housing First, as well as other social programs, although at times may look like giveaways to the poor, they are wise investments.

Welfare for the Rich

As it seems, welfare in America is not just for the poor. Here are a few examples of what corporate lobbying managed to achieve over the years for their clients and what local governments should be cutting back, especially while trying to balance a budget. Some of the largest corporations in the US tend to receive subsidies from various states. For example, GM recently received the most at a total of $1.7 billion. Shell, Ford, and Chrysler all received over $1 billion each. Microsoft, Amazon, Boeing, Prudential, as well as several casino companies in Colorado and New Jersey received over $200 million each.

Of course, many of these subsidies (free money if you will) come from local towns and states that are trying to lure corporations into their local economy or in troubled times prevent them from leaving their local markets. The bad news is that in the end, corporations are always doing whatever they want. For example, in the case of General Motors, during 2009 even after the company received massive subsidies to stay open in certain locations, they still closed those factories anyway. According to *New York Times*, in 2009 fifty properties on the liquidation list were in states that had awarded incentives adding up to billions of taxpayer dollars. In the case of GM, thanks to a federal bailout, the company once more is profitable. The towns and states have not been so fortunate, though, having to invest a significant portion of their capital in exchange for thousands of jobs that no longer exist. The *New York Times* analysis shows that some states are found to be spending between 20 percent and 35 percent of their annual budgets on these subsidies, while Texas, at $19 billion a year, awards more than in any other state. The Cato Institute estimates that financial assistance to corporations cost taxpayers almost $100 billion annually. And as if subsidies (free money) alone were not good enough, special tax breaks allow for corporations to reduce their taxes from a 35 percent tax rate to a lower tax rate of only 13 percent, thus enabling them to keep an additional $200 billion in their pockets each year.

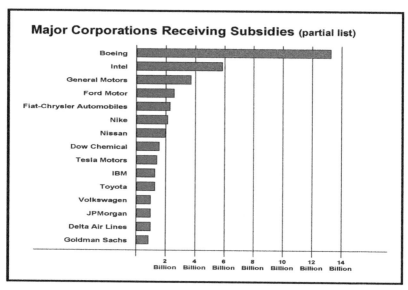

And more loopholes help the rich avoid paying their fair share in taxes. For example, federal tax breaks for wealthy hedge fund managers (those who invest other people's money for a fee) allow them to pay only a 15 percent rate on their profits, while the people they earned money for pay the standard 35 percent rate. This is the tax break where the multimillionaire money managers base their taxes on a lower tax rate than their own secretaries. It is because hedge fund managers can classify some of their income as capital gains (investment income), which means that even though they earn millions of dollars in profit, they only pay a special low tax. Needless to say, those who benefit from this tax loophole are extremely wealthy individuals on Wall Street who are making millions of dollars of profit by using billions of other people's money to invest. In 2013, it was estimated that the federal government lost $83 billion in tax revenue just from this tax loophole.

The federal mortgage reduction loophole, which costs taxpayers an additional $70 billion each year must also be reformed.

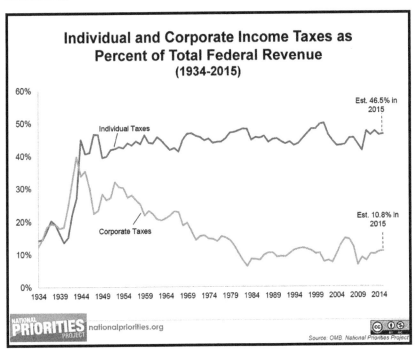

Tax credits to established oil and gas companies also must be abolished. These subsidies were originally meant for emerging industries and businesses that needed assistance to break into the market. Strangely, though, while the largest oil and gas companies in the US not only have broken into the market a long time ago, at present, while they are the most profitable, they continue to benefit from Section 199 of the US Tax Code.

According to data from the US Energy Information Administration, from 2007 to 2009, the top US oil and gas companies paid income taxes based on a reduced rate of 25 percent rather than the standard federal corporate tax rate of 35 percent. The lower rate allowed these few companies to pocket an extra $4 billion yearly and taxpayers to lose a total of $12 billion over the noted three-year period.

The Oil Depletion Allowance tax credit essentially allows oil and gas companies to treat oil in the ground as capital equipment! According to the current US Tax Code, the law was created to help lower the overall startup costs of new energy companies and assist them in establishing themselves. This allowance is another loophole that allows established oil companies today to deduct 15 percent of their profits before paying income taxes. It is estimated that eliminating this loophole will save the United States over $1 billion per year.

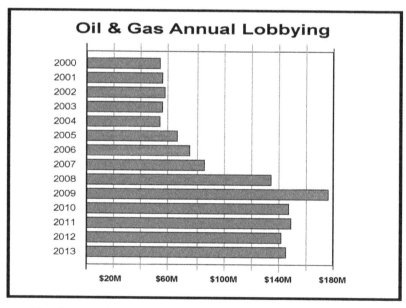

Finally, leaders of huge corporations who engage in wrongful activities should not be allowed to buy their way out of jail, and most importantly, substantial fines often imposed by the federal government should not be allowed to be treated as tax deductions by those corporations. For instance, Reuters reported that JPMorgan Chase, which made a $13 billion mortgage settlement with the federal government, was allowed to write off a majority of the deal as a tax deduction, saving the corporation $4 billion in taxes (just in this case alone).

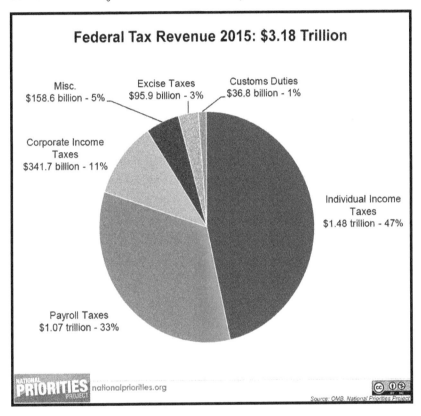

When British Petroleum settled with the US government for the oil catastrophe in the Gulf of Mexico, out of a $37.5 billion penalty, they were allowed to write off and make a deduction of $10 billion. According to an inquiry by the Government Accountability Office, in recent years, twenty out of thirty-four companies that had reached settlements larger than $1 billion reported deducting some or all the penalty amount. That totals to another $20 billion or more. Wonder how many regular people can do the same (deduct from their taxes the cost of their traffic violations and other court fines) and get away with it?

War on Drugs

On a more controversial note, several studies indicate that there may be a better way for the United States to handle the war on drugs and in the process save substantial amounts of money. It has been estimated that since 1971, when Richard Nixon proclaimed drug abuse public enemy number one, the US had spent more than 1 trillion dollars enforcing the law. Unfortunately, though, the same studies also show that, as in the case of prohibition, the United States has nothing to show for this enormous investment. Is it possible there is an alternative to fighting illegal drugs and substance abuse?

In 1925, H. L. Mencken wrote an impassioned plea regarding prohibition. He said,

> *"Five years of Prohibition have had, at least, this one benign effect. They have completely disposed of all the favorite arguments of the Prohibitionists. None of the great boons and usufructs that were to follow the passage of the Eighteenth Amendment has come to pass. There is not less drunkenness in the Republic, but more. There is not less crime, but more. There is not less insanity, but more. The cost of government is not smaller, but vastly larger. Respect for law has not increased, but diminished."*

There is little doubt that Mencken's plea could easily apply to today's policy on illegal drugs. Just as prohibition brought more consumption of hard liquor in the United States, which was produced and distributed by organized crime, similarly, today the number of illegal drug users in the United States and around the world has risen dramatically. Today, the United Nations estimates that there are 230 million users worldwide. The good news is that they also classified 90 percent of these as non-problematic.

In 1980, when the US declared the war on drugs, out of 501,000 incarcerated Americans, 41,000 were in jail for drug use, less than 10 percent of the prison population. Today, there are 2.3 million imprisoned people in the US and 501,500, nearly 25 percent of the inmate population, are serving time for drug offenses. So have the extreme measures taken in the last forty years to reduce drug use worked? Obviously not! Just as with prohibition, banning alcohol did not work, the war on drugs did not work either. If anything, excessive laws, even on the smallest offenses, overpopulated an already crowded prison system and ruined many lives.

A Pew study concluded that the average cost to keep an inmate incarcerated is $30,000 annually. When multiplying the cost of incarceration by five hundred thousand inmates, the number of people in prison with light drug offenses, it becomes clear that local governments are spending $15 billion a year to keep these individuals in jail. The US also spends an additional $41 billion a year to enforce the ineffective laws on drugs.

In contrast, recognizing the nature of this problem, several countries in recent years reversed their drug laws and decriminalized the use of light drugs. In many of these countries, drug addiction is now treated like any other addiction. Rather than investing their money in incarcerating the drug users, these countries spend their money in educating and helping drug addicts to break their habits.

For example, in 2001, Portugal decriminalized the use of all drugs, including marijuana, cocaine, heroin, and others! While, of course, drugs in Portugal are still considered illegal, today under the new law, authorities view the possession and use of small quantities of drugs as a public health issue, not a criminal one. Portuguese authorities no longer arrest anyone holding up to a ten-day supply of an illegal drug. Instead, they issue a citation. Drug offenders with repeat citations are required to go before a panel of legal, social, and psychological experts. Many cases are merely suspended, while others, depending on the panel's opinion, require the individual to undergo treatment, which can vary from drug counseling to therapy.

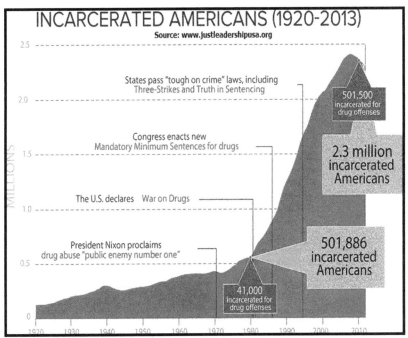

The rate of incarcerated Americans (held in prison for using illegal drugs) steadily rose from 10 percent in 1980 to an all-time high of 25 percent in 2013.

When Portugal decided to decriminalize drugs, skeptics argued that the number of drug users would skyrocket. However, in the past fifteen years, the rate of drug addicts fell and is now slightly below other European nations. The percentage of drug-related HIV infections also steadily dropped since 2001, and drug-induced deaths dropped down to 3 per 1 million people, a mortality rate that is fifteen times lower than in other

European countries, and fifty times lower than that of the United States (see chart below). Moreover, as the stigma of using drugs was removed, more people in Portugal looked for care to treat their addiction. Out of 100,000 people known to be habitual users of heavy drugs, 50,000 of them are currently going through treatment to cure their addiction.

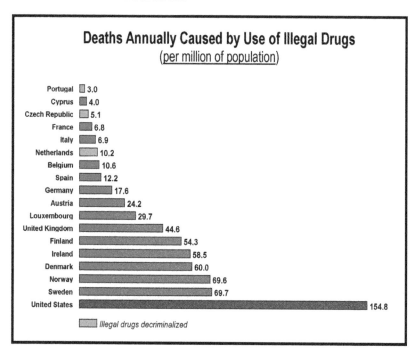

Another nation known as the one with the most relaxed drug laws is the Netherlands. Most people don't realize, though, that in Netherlands — except for few soft drugs, which are highly regulated by the government — all other drugs are considered forbidden and illegal. The Netherlands Opium Act, which covers all the hard drugs under Schedule 1 (drugs such as opium, cocaine, amphetamines, heroin, etc.) prohibits the production, possession, use, sale, import, or export of these drugs. Conversely, soft drugs under Schedule 2 (such as marijuana and hashish) are legalized and are allowed to be sold through licensed shops. These "coffee shops" are allowed to sell 5 grams of cannabis to a person per day.

With respect to the Netherlands' drug policies, as in the case of Portugal, critics feared that distribution of soft drugs would be a stimulator for further use or that it could lead the path to hard drugs. These concerns, as was the case in Portugal, were proven wrong. Cannabis consumption also did not explode out of control but instead averages the same as in any other country. As for the fear that consumption of hard drugs will rise, that did not happen either. The level of those in the Netherlands who use cocaine and other hard drugs is slightly lower than in other countries.

Regarding money, while the Netherlands still spends a good amount enforcing its illegal drug policies, it is worth noting that it generates an additional $500 million in taxes annually, an amount that is invested back into the system for addiction prevention and treatment.

If the United States adopted similar measures as did the Netherlands, decriminalizing marijuana and other illegal soft drugs and then regulate and tax at rates comparable to those on alcohol and tobacco, the local governments could potentially yield $46 billion annually. A Cato study shows that legalizing drugs would also save the US another $41 billion per year from enforcing the drug laws. When combining the savings from incarceration ($15 billion), law enforcement, and taxation, local governments in the United States could conceivably collect an additional $102 billion per year.

PART 3
Making a Difference

Making America Great Again

William Greider in his book *The Soul of Capitalism* wrote:

> *"What Americans should by now be able to see is that neither the laissez-faire marketplace, nor strong government has given them a satisfying or permanent resolution. The problem is not the marketplace, and it is not government. The problem originates in the contest of clashing values between society and capitalism and, since this human society cannot surrender its deepest values, it must try to alter capitalism's. As we look deeper for the soul of capitalism, we find that, in the terms of ordinary human existence, American capitalism doesn't appear to have one."*

Well said, considering that the needs of people are vastly different than that of a corporation's. By nature, corporations care less about the environment, education, unemployment, starvation, disease, homelessness, or for that matter, their own workforce. To big businesses, people are a means to an end. All that matters is a high bottom line number. To prosper, they require a dynamic market, open borders, and the ability to carry out their business as they please and where they please. Principles do not bind them, and their only loyalty is to their investors. When it comes to politics, corporations always choose to support those in government who favor their wants over the needs of their workers or consumers. In fact, organized corporate lobbying serves no other purpose but to have elected politicians implement the company's needs first even if those could be against the needs of the average American.

In a televised address on July 6, 1976, Ronald Reagan said the following:

> "I'm convinced that today the majority of Americans want what those first Americans wanted: A better life for themselves and their children; a minimum of government authority. Very simply, they want to be left alone in peace and safety to take care of the family by earning an honest dollar and putting away some savings. This may not sound too exciting, but there is something magnificent about it. On the farm, on the street corner, in the factory and in the kitchen, millions of us ask nothing more, but certainly nothing less than to live our own lives according to our values – at peace with ourselves, our neighbors and the world."

A lot have changed, though, in the last forty years. Today, in a not-so-perfect globalized world where corporate interests rule, and the needs of millions of people are often brushed aside for the sake of higher profits, how can Ronald Reagan's simplistic vision work? In an unregulated open-border free market, human needs and corporate wants are bound to clash. In an environment where conglomerate interests are placed above the needs of society by elected politicians, the mighty corporations will always have the advantage, unless of course people recognize this flaw in the system and begin to demand more for themselves.

Once upon a time, joining trade unions was the best way for the average American worker to secure a good-paying job and a way to earn and save that "honest dollar" Ronald Reagan spoke of. Today, with no unions or a government that represents the ordinary worker, and with all the power in the hands of big corporations, Americans rely solely on their buying power to reward or punish particular business practices. In a system where there is no oversight in how employers manage their workforce, consumers often tend to support companies who care for their workers and punish those who don't by not buying their products or services. And while this practice may eventually force companies to notice and become more socially responsible, apparently this is not enough to make a difference.

To make a difference, Americans must arise once more and claim back their country by using the one tool they are left with—their vote! Rather than blindly vote for the party of their ideology, though, or allow for the often one-sided corporate-controlled media influence their judgment, Americans should learn to set divisive politics aside and vote for qualified politicians who sincerely encourage dialogue and unity in Washington. Most importantly, they should support those who understand that a thriving economy cannot be solely measured by corporate success on Wall Street but also by the number of people on Main Street who can earn real living wages and at the end of the day have some disposable income to invest back into the market.

A closer examination of the American economy reveals that the most significant problem Americans face today is the fact that over the last forty-five years, salaries and hourly wages have either remained stagnant or have declined significantly. If the minimum wage nearly five decades ago allowed $3/hour more disposable income than the minimum wage today, and today, after nearly five decades, 44 percent of all Americans work for less than $10 an hour (essentially less than the minimum wage in 1968), this presents a serious problem not only for the American consumer but for the American economy as well. No wonder 75 million Americans today feel disgruntled, not to mention forsaken, by the very economic system they help support. In the last few decades, stagnating wages, in contrast to soaring corporate profits on Wall Street, and the neglect or failure by politicians to understand the real needs of the average American, not to mention the unwarranted and ongoing political gridlock in Washington DC, is the real reason why in recent presidential elections, tens of millions of Americans supported non-seasoned politicians. The big irony, though, is that over the same period, while Americans were searching for their ideal representative to clean up Washington, large corporations continued to lobby and pay poverty wages, thus forcing more and more working people into the welfare system. All the while, organized propaganda, through the corporate-controlled media, managed to promote the idea that the less fortunate on the pay scale, those who now rely on government assistance, are the real problem behind America's economic woes. And all this at the very time when huge corporations and many billionaires, via "special" tax loopholes, kept undermining the American economy by paying little or no taxes.

In a system where the worker payroll and individual taxes combined make up more than 80 percent of the entire federal tax revenue, while corporate tax contribution is down to an all-time low of 9.9 percent and shrinking, it should not be considered inapt for the average American worker to expect occasional financial assistance or, for that matter, more benefits for themselves and their families from the very system they wholly support. Or is the system rigged in such a way that only big corporations and wealthy individuals (corporate executives and Wall Street moguls) may exert influence in Washington DC? How is it possible that corporate tax evasion, a legal or not so legal one, is praised by the media today as a smart business practice, but when an average individual who pays taxes asks for more from the very system he or she solely supports, that person is labeled as a moocher?

If companies are set up only to make profits and not to solve America's problems, and the US government as expected is to remain neutral, in that case, who is left to look out for the needs of the average American other than people themselves? So in addition to other social services today taken for granted, such as social security benefits, Medicare, Medicaid, etc., is it absurd for the average American to also expect, as in other wealthy nations, "free" universal health care as well as "free" (or reasonably priced) higher education, especially since today the latter, as we are told, is a prerequisite for assured employment and better-paying jobs? And why not? Instead, in the last ten years, substantial federal cuts in higher education led to massive increases in school tuition, which drove student loan debt to skyrocket. The cost of higher education has surged more than 500 percent since 1985. In essence, a $20,000 education in 1985 costs over $100,000 today.

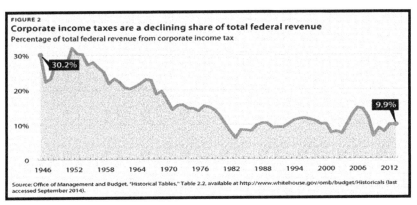

FIGURE 2
Corporate income taxes are a declining share of total federal revenue
Percentage of total federal revenue from corporate income tax

Source: Office of Management and Budget, "Historical Tables," Table 2.2, available at http://www.whitehouse.gov/omb/budget/Historicals (last accessed September 2014).

According to the Federal Reserve Bank of New York, since 2004, outstanding student loans quadrupled to $1.2 trillion, leaving roughly 40 million Americans trapped with a debt often too high to repay. And while most Americans don't quite understand why this debt is an imminent threat to the US economy, the truth is, rising student debt is changing how tens of millions of Americans approach major personal and financial decisions in their lives. Due to their high debt, many of these people are postponing marriage, childbirth, buying houses, cars, or even starting small businesses, all things that make an economy grow. To make matters even worse, the tuition debt at graduation for many of these students is so high, with half of their income going toward their education loans, many of them are forced to rely on government assistance (or their parents) to make ends meet. Today, according to the Census Bureau, 22 million young adults in the 18–34 age bracket (one out of every three) live at home with their parents as they cannot afford to be on their own. The same study also shows that the number of young Americans relying on their parents increased by 8 million since 1975. That comes as no surprise, though, since the median income for this age group in 1975 was $10,000 higher (see chart on page 28), while the cost of education was five times cheaper (see chart below). In effect, every time politicians underfund higher education for the sake of other programs, not only does this encourage tuition rates to climb higher, but as a result, this hurt the economy by forcing more and more young adults to turn to the government or their parents for financial assistance.

Eventually, Americans must realize that investing in making higher education cheaper, if not free for everyone, is ultimately more beneficial for the society as well as for the economy than the current alternative, which is investing in the ever-increasing cost of social programs.

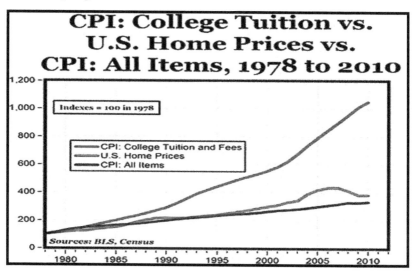

CPI: College Tuition vs. U.S. Home Prices vs. CPI: All Items, 1978 to 2010

Indexes = 100 in 1978

CPI: College Tuition and Fees
U.S. Home Prices
CPI: All Items

Sources: BLS, Census

As for health care, in the case of a serious illness, when comparing the status quo to a free universal health-care system, wouldn't an early diagnosis and preventive treatment by a nonprofit system cost the taxpayer much less? Unquestionably, free medical care would encourage most people to see their doctor regularly. That, in turn, could help identify and prevent many conditions that often — in the current system, where millions of people and especially the uninsured find it too expensive to see a doctor — go unnoticed until they turn life-threatening and financially catastrophic. And in the end, what happens when the sick cannot afford their enormous for-profit treatment? As always, other consumers help cover those losses with higher-than-ever health-care premiums.

Funding for free universal health care and higher education can be obtained in part from the substantial profits the pharmaceutical, health-care, and insurance providers are making while these services are privatized. (According to the Center for Public Integrity, out of a total annual revenue of $130.5 billion, in 2015, health-care insurers alone profited $10.3 billion, a record high profit for the industry.) Funds for these essential services can also be found within the enormous financial waste employed by the federal government. An examination of the federal budget shows that politics aside, the federal government could not only fund these programs but still have enough cash in reserve to balance the budget. Finally, additional money could be generated by eliminating the corporate tax loopholes that allow profit-shifting overseas, and by forcing American companies to begin paying taxes in the US and not to some other tax haven country.

When politicians cry that America has trouble balancing its annual budget, should the American taxpayers automatically subject themselves to more sacrifices or expressly ask that politicians first "sharpen their pencils" and further demand that hundreds of American corporations, who are now purposely bending the rules and hold trillions of dollars in offshore accounts in order to avoid paying taxes, should repatriate their income and finally pay Uncle Sam their dues?

On March 2016, the *Washington Post* reported that US companies currently hold $2.4 trillion overseas to avoid paying $695 billion in taxes. And that is not all! Several more locally based companies choose to shift their profits to other countries, where taxes are much lower. According to the same source, several American companies based in the US are now saving over $100 billion in taxes every year by shifting their profits overseas!

The American public must no longer tolerate this massive corporate tax evasion and demand that the elected representatives pass legislation to eliminate all loopholes that allow for this tax dodging to go on, and force these companies, whether based here or abroad, to pay and to continue to pay their taxes (as it is generally required from individuals with any overseas income). Furthermore, through legislation, Americans should demand that either big corporations decrease their dominance over the federal government or increase their responsibility and allegiance to America.

If European countries, such as the small island of Cyprus, for instance, with only one million in population, can afford to provide their citizens with free health care as well as free higher education, not to mention worker benefits inconceivable to the ordinary American (see chart USA versus Cyprus on page 85), is that because foreign governments know better how to manage money? Or as in the case of Cyprus, this is possible because Walmart, Goldman Sachs, Kellogg, JPMorgan Chase and Co., along with hundreds of other American corporations, choose to pay their tribute to Cyprus and other tax-haven countries instead of paying their taxes in the United States, where taxes are due.

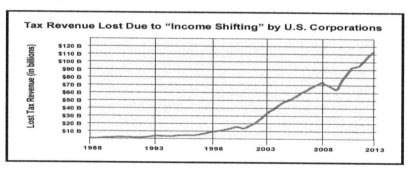

Goldman Sachs, for example, has 987 subsidiaries in twenty tax-haven countries. Two of these subsidiaries are located in Cyprus, while another 537 of those (never mind that these branches could be just mailbox addresses) are in the Cayman Islands! Goldman Sachs currently holds more than 28 billion dollars in tax-haven countries. Walmart is another such company. Without an actual store in either Cyprus or Luxembourg, the company claims one subsidiary in Cyprus and twenty-two more in Luxembourg. To avoid paying taxes in the US, Walmart currently holds more than 77 billion dollars in various offshore accounts.

The comparison below, between United States and Cyprus, is based on a household of a married couple (no children), earning a combined annual income of $55,000, with two cars, and a house valued up to $200,000.

USA	ANNUAL INCOME VS. LIVING COSTS	CYPRUS[2]
$55,000	**INCOME (ANNUALLY)**	**$55,000**
	TAXES/INSURANCE	
$7,000	*Federal Taxes*	*$0*
$2,700	*State Taxes*	*$0*
7%	*Sales Tax]/[Consumption Tax*	*19%*
$2,000	*Annual Real Estate Tax (Avg.)*	*$0*
$800	*Real Estate Insurance (Avg.)*	*$0*
$2,500	*Car Insurance (Avg.)*	*$600*
$7,600 (+co-pays)	*Health Insurance (Avg.)*	*$0*
$27,600	**Net Pay (Before Consumption)**	**$54,400**
	OTHER MAJOR DIFFERENCES	
$75,000+	*Cost of Higher education*	*$0*
$400+	*Est. cost of co-pays*	*$0 **
$ 600 +	*Prescription drug cost*	*$150 +*
$ 150 +	*Emergency Room Visit*	*$0 **
	WORK AND BENEFITS MANDATED BY GOV'T	
40	*Hours of Work per Week*	*40*
0	*Paid Vacation/ Total Days*	*28 days*
0	*Paid Holidays/ Total Days*	*7 days*
0	*Maternity Leave/ Paid*	*126 days*
0	*Maternity Leave/ Unpaid*	*+91 days*
0	*Paternity Leave/ Paid*	*49 days*
0	*Salary Bonus*	*1 Month*
0	*Severance Pay*	*1/2M per*
0	*Sick Days Paid/ Light Illness (flu)*	*3 Days*
0	*Sick Days Paid/ Serious Illness*	*182 Days*
39%	CORPORATE TAXES	12.5% Flat

---

2   *Regarding its political system, Cyprus, just as the United States, is a republic. With a European-style democracy, it strongly upholds individual rights while encour-*

Europe, apparently, is not only known for its remarkable benefits to the employed but also for offering impressive benefits to the unemployed as well. Europeans are known to get higher unemployment compensation and for much longer time. For example, in the US, depending on the particular state, unemployment benefits typically range between $350 and $450 per week, for up to six months at a time, regardless of one's previous income level. According to *Forbes* magazine, the small country of Luxembourg pays as much as 80 percent of one's former income,

---

aging free enterprise. In fact, the island's economy is remarkably prosperous and very much resembles that of the United States, with one significant difference. The median wealth (personal net worth) in Cyprus, at 266,900 euros ($311,000+/-), is considered to be one of the highest in the world (roughly six times higher than that of the United States or Germany). Of course, the reasons why Cypriots can accumulate wealth faster than the average American is demonstrated in this particular comparison. For example, no income taxes on a combined income of up to $55,000 provides a great start to accumulate wealth (income up to $55,000 in Cyprus is considered living income). A married couple in Cyprus is expected to pay only $2,000 in taxes for every additional income of $10,000 earned above $55,000.

Health care as well as public education, including college education, is free to all Cypriot citizens provided they go to a local university.

Private health-care insurance exists primarily for those who wish to skip the occasional long line or expect the VIP treatment of a private room instead of sharing a room with others. Needless to say, private health care is much more affordable since physicians must compete with a free health-care system. To see a private physician typically costs around $20. An emergency visit to the hospital (regardless of one's medical condition or citizenship) is free of charge, and that goes for tourists and citizens of other countries while living and working on the island (medical care is viewed as a human right). Houses with an estimated value of up to $200,000 (170,860 euros) are tax exempt. Owners of larger more-expensive homes pay property taxes but only a fraction in comparison to the taxes paid in the US. With respect to tax revenue, the significant difference between the two countries is that United States relies heavily on income taxes, while Cyprus generates its tax income primarily from a consumption tax of 19 percent (the VAT system is a tax similar to the fair tax proposed in the US). The 19 percent consumption tax applies to all goods except food. Of course, additional income is generated from all the wealthier households who earn more than $55,000 annually. It is also worth mentioning that the 12.5 percent flat corporate tax, which is one of the lowest corporate tax rates in the world, brings additional tax revenue even from foreign companies. (With a low 12.5 percent corporate tax, Cyprus is considered a tax-haven country to many international companies. Walmart, for example, is one among several American and European companies that have registered subsidiaries in Cyprus to avoid paying higher taxes in their country of origin.)

while Denmark pays 90 percent. (And while for many Americans this appears to be too cushy, according to the IMF, the unemployment rate in Denmark is only 3.9 percent.) Many other European countries pay their unemployed between 40 percent and 70 percent of their previous regular wages for a period of up to twenty months or even longer in some special cases.

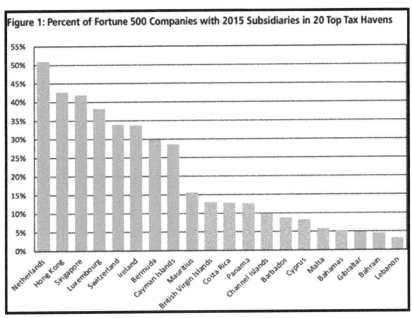

Figure 1: Percent of Fortune 500 Companies with 2015 Subsidiaries in 20 Top Tax Havens

So if American corporate taxes help in part to finance some of the generous public programs that 500 million Europeans today depend upon, is it absurd for Americans to also expect the very same type of benefits for themselves, especially since the enormous tax revenue American companies pay overseas rightfully belongs to US taxpayers? We must also not overlook the fact that while many of these corporations choose to shift their taxes overseas, their profits are often made on US soil while exploiting American workers with poverty wages and no benefits of any kind. How is that fair to the average US worker?

INCOME TAXES & BENEFITS - USA VS. OTHER COUNTRIES

	Germany	Italy	UK	France	Cyprus	USA
TAXES						
Taxes on annual income of $27,500	15%	23%	20%	14%	0	15%
Consumption Tax (Sales Tax or VAT)	19%	22%	20%	20%	19%	7%
HEALTHCARE						
Cost of healthcare/ Annually	Free	Free	Free	Free	Free	$7,600
COLLEGE TUITION						
Cost of higher education/ Annually	Free	$1,000	$4,000	$200	Free	$9,410
EMPLOYEE BENEFITS (Mandated by the government)						
Hours work per week	35	40	40	35	40	40
Paid Vacation/ Days per Year	24	20	20	20	28	0
Paid National Holidays/ Days per year	10	13	0	11	7	0
Maternity Leave/ PAID (Days per Year)	329	175	91	154	126	0
Maternity Leave/ UNPAID (Additional days to paid leave)	861	308	469	2072	91	0
Paternity Leave PAID (Days per Year)	63	7	14	11	7	0
Annual Pay Bonus (Additional Salary)	1 Month	1 Month	0	0	1 Month	0
Severance Pay with Termination of Employment	1/2M per YR	4-24 Months	$17,575	1/5M per YR	1M every 2 YRs	0
Sick Days Paid Annually (Common Illness)	5	1	0	1	3	0
Sick Days Paid Annually (Uncommon Illness, Surgery, etc)	44	29	10	24	182	0
FOR BUSINESS/ CORPORATIONS						
Corporate Tax	30%	27.5%	22%	34%	12.5% Flat	39.1%

It is worth mentioning that just about every political system, whether that is capitalism, socialism, communism, autocracy or democracy, all employ social programs to improve their people's lives and especially the lives of the less fortunate. Those Americans who worry that social programs in effect could ultimately change capitalism into socialism don't quite realize that public services alone are not classifying a society, but rather, they characterize the degree of its civilization.

In the case of capitalism, for instance, the following public programs are deemed acceptable: Social Security income, Medicare, Medicaid, Unemployment Insurance, Supplemental Security Income (assistance to low-income seniors, the blind, or disabled), Earned Income Tax Credit (EITC), the Federal Pell Grant (a student aid program), Temporary Assistance for Needy Families (TANF), Child Care Assistance Program (CCAP), Child Nutrition Program (CHIP), the Section 8 rental subsidy, and the Welfare Assistance Program. Aren't all these some sort of social programs? In fact, aren't police, public schools and public libraries forms of social services as well? Of course, they are. Whether these programs are funded on a local or a federal level, all are financed by the taxpayer for the good of the community. So if "social welfare" policy is defined as an act, law, a program, or a service that aims to improve the lives of people in the community, shouldn't one of those acts funded by taxpayer money also ensured that all taxpayers were covered under the Medicaid program? Why (among all the other social programs already in place) is free universal health care often labeled as socialism? Can it be perhaps because it goes against the special interests of the private insurance companies?

As for the typical concern that Medicaid for all would put the insurance industry out of business, to ease those fears, as in other countries, private insurance companies will most likely continue to sell fancy health-care policies offering ultra-premium coverage and plans geared to pamper the most affluent Americans.

With respect to the current political system and gridlock of "politics as usual," Americans should demand that politicians, just like US presidents, begin to serve limited terms too. Only when politicians, in both the Senate and the House, stop making entire careers in politics they will begin to think less about their own political future and more about how to best serve their country and their constituents. Moreover, to help reduce the influence lobbying currently has over Washington, there should be a law that prohibits politicians from becoming lobbyists, or in any capacity serve a lobbying company, within five to ten years after they finish their term in office. When elected politicians over a thirty- or forty-year political career collect hundreds of thousands of dollars to help them retain their political positions, in the end, to whom will they most likely be loyal to, the voters who initially elected them but invested nothing on them or the number of businesses that supported them financially over time with millions in campaign contributions?

Table 2: Top 30 Companies with the Most Money Held Offshore

Company	Amount Held Offshore ($ millions)	Number of Tax Haven Subsidiaries	Company	Amount Held Offshore ($ millions)	Number of Tax Haven Subsidiaries
Apple	214,900	3	PepsiCo	40,200	135
Pfizer	193,587	181	J.P. Morgan Chase & Co.	34,600	385
Microsoft	124,000	5	Amgen	32,600	9
General Electric	104,000	20	Coca-Cola	31,900	15
International Business Machines	68,100	16	United Technologies	29,000	31
Merck	59,200	125	Qualcomm	28,800	3
Google	58,300	1	Goldman Sachs Group	28,550	987
Cisco Systems	58,000	56	Gilead Sciences	28,500	12
Johnson & Johnson	58,000	62	Intel	26,900	13
Exxon Mobil	51,000	35	Eli Lilly	26,500	33
Procter & Gamble	49,000	35	Walmart	26,100	
Hewlett-Packard	47,200	95	AbbVie Inc	25,000	38
Chevron	45,400	8	Bristol-Myers Squibb	25,000	23
Citigroup	45,200	140	Danaher	23,500	31
Oracle	42,600	5	Philip Morris International	23,000	7
			Total:	**1,648,637**	**2,509**

In summary, disenfranchised Americans on both sides of the aisle must realize that their future and the future of America is solely in their hands, and no particular political ideology, an elected politician, or any presidential candidate without overwhelming public pressure and support can ever bring real change to this country. In an environment where votes are in short supply and cable "news" organizations overtly are "selling" one political dogma over another, to avoid being influenced in any way, vigilant voters should learn to switch these propaganda channels off.

Most Americans today think of propaganda simply as a tactic used in war to influence people's attitudes. What they do not realize, though, is that they are also subjected to it daily by newspapers, television, radio, social media, and by all other means of communication. According to the dictionary, *propaganda* is biased information used to promote a particular political ideology or a point of view, in effect, exactly what the left- and right-wing media organizations do 24/7. As they say, those who control the media have access to and potentially control public opinion. In other words, talk and opinion shows masquerading as the news should no longer be acknowledged or internalized. Are shows with friendly or not-so-friendly anchors offering their assessment and thoughts during news broadcasts, monologue acts, commentaries, or news programs with a typical panel of "experts," a group of two, three, or more individuals discussing and analyzing even live broadcasts, really the news or the opinion of those people? What is the purpose of so much assessment and opinion mixed with the daily news anyhow other than to promote one view or another? Even more importantly, how does this type of "programming" affect the audience over time? One thing is clear. In the past two decades, Americans have become extremely polarized in their political and personal opinions more than ever before. Nowadays, not only do they disagree on their political views, but they also profoundly disagree on common-sense everyday matters. Over time, attitudes, beliefs, and behaviors have drastically changed, depending on one's choice of news supply, and the situation is getting worse. So who truly benefits from this unwholesome division? The media? The politicians? The corporations? Perhaps all of the above? Certainly not the American public, the victim in this situation.

Americans, both Republicans and Democrats, must come together against a media propaganda system that in the last twenty years has grown more sophisticated in the art of perception management and must attempt to rescue America from becoming a managed democracy (a nation controlled by the privileged, special interests, and corporations).

In his book *How Propaganda Works*, scholar Jason Stanley, a professor of philosophy at Yale University, explains,

> *"Propaganda is characteristically part of the mechanism by which people become deceived about how best to realize their goals, and hence deceived from seeing what is in their own best interests."*

This, he further explains, is achieved

- *by appealing to the emotions in such a way that rational debate is sidelined or short-circuited*
- *by promoting an insider/outsider dynamic that pollutes the broader conversation with negative stereotypes of out-of-favor groups, and*
- *by eroding community standards of reasonableness that depend on norms of mutual respect and mutual accountability.*

With propaganda, he also notes, "Innocent words can take negative connotations as they become imbued, by a mechanism of repeated association with problematic images or stereotypes." According to Mr. Stanley, propaganda "thrives in a polarized environment in which truth is regarded as relativistic and facts are treated as interchangeable with fantasy."

In short, propaganda (a psychological campaign circulated by the mass media with the intent to promote a political agenda, an ideology, or a point of view), uses biased or misleading information, which aims to manipulate people's emotions in order to influence their opinions and ultimately shape their attitudes, beliefs, and behavior. Of course, in addition to just tapping into people's emotions by the use of images and slogans, propaganda also works by selective use of information and censorship of the facts, something some governments do before and during war campaigns. As a matter of fact, to convince the public to take up arms, a state-sponsored propaganda can result in even more sinister methods. Hitler's propaganda chief, Herman Goering (during the Nuremberg trials), could not have explained this any better:

> *Of course the people don't want war. But after all, it's the leaders of the country who determine the policy, and it's always a simple matter to drag the people along, whether it's a democracy, a fascist dictatorship, or a parliament, or a communist dictatorship. Voice or no voice, the people can always be brought to the bidding of the leaders. That is easy. All you have to do is tell them they are being attacked, and denounce the pacifists for lack of patriotism and exposing the country to greater danger.*

A disturbing tactic, indeed, especially since the ploy above can easily be used today on the exceedingly polarized American public!

It is no secret that in the last twenty years, with the aid of the cable news media, politicians managed to divide the country into two political sides. This harmful division allows the mass media to take political propaganda to a whole new level. No longer does propaganda promote one political ideology over another. These days, with the public deeply divided and susceptible to persuasion more than ever before, partisan cable news organizations get away with even more extreme "programming" which aims not only to alter the worldview of their audience but literally crash all those they oppose by blaming the opposition for all that is wrong today. Attacking the opposition and disintegrating the rival party's values, ideas, and beliefs deep in their core is now the new standard in American politics, while compromising on the various issues for the country's sake is no longer an option.

This ongoing psychological campaign on the American public, not to mention the current economic conditions, explains why many Americans today become angry or irritated when discussing politics. An *Esquire*/NBC survey taken in January 2016 found that half of all Americans at the time felt angrier than in the previous year. The study also noted that while people are angry, they tend to be poor listeners. They demonstrate little empathy and have trouble understanding other people's views. In other words, as the two political parties grow angrier with each other over time, it becomes harder for American voters to find a common ground and to begin fixing America's problems. The sad part is that regardless of the emotions and the apparent differences between the two political ideologies, most Americans, when "not under influence," genuinely agree on the majority of the issues. Every American wants to improve the economy, fight terrorism, reduce the budget deficit, reduce health-care costs, stabilize the social security system, improve education, and ultimately cultivate a better and safer future for themselves and their families. If only the news media adhered to journalism and politicians placed their country above party.

Likely, as experts say, education and brainwashing do not work hand in hand. Being well informed can help one see all sides of an issue. Using more logic, less emotion, accepting no opinions, questioning everything, and ignoring popular beliefs also help. Finally, obtaining the "daily news" from a variety of media sources (by alternating and equally watching left- and right-wing news networks) may ultimately help one recognize and separate the real information from the propaganda.

In conclusion, in a post-truth age when Americans cast their votes, hoping to restore the American Dream, they must remember that by placing their needs, their family's needs, and the needs of their fellow citizens above the special interests in the current state of affairs, is how they can neutralize the power of corporate lobbying, fight against propaganda, and begin to "Make America Great Again" for everyone!

Conclusion

No country on this planet can ever achieve greatness as long as the happiness and welfare of its people are only measured in money. Money without health is not possible as one must be healthy to be truly happy. As Virgil, a great Roman poet, once wrote, "The greatest wealth is health."

While, as expected, many young adults in their twenties may disagree with Virgil, when asking older people in their fifties what they would choose if they had a choice between an increase in pay or a free universal health care, most would say health care. It is no big surprise that people's life expectations and views ultimately change with age.

Today, out of 7 billion people in the world, more than 2 billion of them, roughly one-third, are over the age of fifty. America, in that respect, is no different from the rest of the world. In fact, nearly 110 million Americans (one out of every three) are currently over the age of fifty, and according to the AARP, this number will grow by another 10 million just in the next three years alone. To all these middle-aged Americans, a good health-care system today may be more important than money. It is for that very same reason why thousands of older Americans are holding jobs, so they reap the benefits of an employer-sponsored health-care coverage.

The United States, a remaining country in a group of industrialized nations, still trades its health care for profit. The truth is, in the past ten to fifteen years, health-care premiums, as well as treatment costs in the US, have gotten so much out of control that health care is now beginning to affect the country's economy. Elected officials on both sides of the aisle have finally recognized the problem, but as it appears, they remain unable to fix it. Sadly, in American politics, politicians seem to place party above country. How this will affect America in the future remains to be seen!

So in the event all efforts to improve the health-care system fail, why don't Americans be more pragmatic and copy the European "free" health-care system? Hundreds of millions of Europeans seem to enjoy it, and as it appears, European nations save a lot of money when it comes to per capita comparisons.

Free health care, though, isn't truly free. Adopting such a solution will require a slight increase in taxes (at a minimum, an amount equal to what employers currently deduct from employees' paychecks to cover the employees' portion of health-care cost). This additional tax will provide the extra funds needed for the current Medicare program to be extended to everyone.

The good news, if this idea ever takes place, is that Americans for the very first time will indeed never worry about pre-existing conditions, deductibles, or complicated treatments. No one ever again will fall into poverty because of a medical condition or due to the rising costs of health care. Equally, no longer will senior citizens force themselves to work just because they need health-care coverage. Free health care for all will certainly free up hundreds of thousands of jobs currently held by older workers to a much younger workforce. And that is not all. The benefits to corporations will be even greater. The fact that businesses will no longer be expected to provide health-care coverage to anyone (which currently it is so expensive that many small companies cannot even afford it) will allow those who now offer it to increase their profit margin and, in essence, recapture the cost of higher pay-rolls as earlier suggested.

Health-care insurance companies, as in other countries, would carry on selling supplemental policies with pampered services geared toward the more affluent citizens and to those who prefer to visit the physician of their choice rather than wait in line for the first available doctor. In the end, as with the status quo, in the case of a catastrophic illness or a complex treatment, all would continue to rely on the very same hospitals currently participating in the Medicare program. Worth mentioning is that all those who would prefer getting additional private health-care coverage will most likely be paying pennies on the dollar as private health-care insurance companies would now be competing with a free health-care system.

With respect to taxation, in addition to implementing a comprehensive personal tax reform, corporate taxes in the US should also be lowered — let's say at a flat rate between 12 and 15 percent (while simultaneously eliminating all corporate loopholes which currently help corporations pay little or no taxes). Although a 12–15 percent flat tax may appear to be too low, in truth, when all other corporate tax loopholes are abolished, this lower rate may increase the overall corporate tax revenue by twofold. Not only would most American companies based abroad be convinced to repatriate their income and continue to pay their fair share of taxes, but thousands of multinational corporations would also be tempted to register subsidiaries and pay taxes in the United States to take advantage of the low rate. Not to mention, there would be no longer a need for home-based companies to shift their profits overseas to save on taxes. If the Netherlands, Luxembourg, Cyprus, and other tax-haven countries successfully operate that way, why wouldn't the United States? Moreover, in exchange for lowering corporate taxes, if a lower tax rate is implemented along with an agreement to raise the minimum wage to a living wage, then the federal government will gain not only from the annual repatriated corporate tax but from the significant reduction in welfare cost since millions of welfare recipients would rise above poverty and would no longer qualify for government assistance.

With respect to higher education, there should be a number of colleges across America subsidized by the US government, where anyone who wants could attend free of charge. So while private renowned universities (such as Yale, Harvard, and others) will always be the schools of choice for the more affluent Americans, free community colleges will help educate the less fortunate without the burden of an enormous debt. As pointed out earlier, massive tuition debt hurts not only those who carry it but, in the long run, hurts the economy as well.

The election process in America must also be reformed. In addition to changing the outdated Electoral College voting system to a system that is based on the majority, casting a vote should also become easier so more people can participate in local and national elections. While officially there are more than 210 million registered voters in the United States today, only about 120 million of those usually cast their vote during a presidential election. Why is that? Voting should be more accessible to anyone who wishes to exercise the right to vote. As in other countries, election days should be carried out as national holidays (a day off with pay), so anyone can take time to vote. Or in this day and age, people should be allowed to vote electronically online, an alternative that will ultimately bring more millennials to the voting booth. After all, millions of financial transactions are taking place daily over the internet, and all are considered to be safe transactions. Filing taxes online also is seen as a safe practice. Every year, out of 137 million tax returns filed in the US, 120 million are being filed electronically without any complications. The IRS proudly claims that it has safely and securely processed more than 1.3 billion e-file tax returns since the online program began. In other words, and regardless of what pundits are saying to the contrary, voting online is not less secure than the current electronic voting methods. Making access to voting easier not only will prompt more registered voters to participate in local and national elections, but this will be the only effective way for Americans to counteract the strong influence the special interests and corporate lobbying have over the federal government.

Finally, and most importantly, the United States must begin to reduce its national debt, which presently hovers at around $20 trillion and growing. Currently, ongoing wars and natural disaster relief efforts (hurricanes, earthquakes, and wildfires) are all funded with borrowed money which continue to add to the debt.

Putting the country on a sustainable fiscal path can create a positive environment for additional economic growth, opportunity, and prosperity. Lowering the debt and providing a strong economic foundation will allow for additional resources for public and private investments needed for America's future; it will improve consumer and business confidence and will provide a stronger financial safety net. Conversely, letting the debt grow will ultimately have several adverse consequences for the economy and will severely impact future policymaking. The confidence in the economic environment will weaken, access to capital will be reduced, and the interest on the debt will begin to drown out essential investments for the country's future. Furthermore, as conditions for growth will continue to deteriorate, the nation's ability to effectively respond to future crises (natural or financial) will be diminished. In short, the rising debt is putting America on the path of another fiscal crisis, one that without money will be much harder to overcome. And that is not all. To make matters worse, the international demand to invest in US assets and US debt, as a portfolio choice, will weaken as the debt level grows.

Currently, due to America's sound economic history of low inflation, low debt, and strong pro-growth policies, there is still global demand to hold US debt. In fact, more than $6 trillion of the federal debt is owned by foreigners. Since the United States continues to provide the world's primary currency for international commerce, this amplifies the demand for US assets, including the debt. As the debt grows, though, the appetite of foreign investors to invest in US debt will decline. (Incidentally, the debt at this time is higher than what America produces in an entire year. Obviously, this high debt-to-GDP ratio indicates to investors, foreign and domestic, that the country might have problems repaying its obligations. An alarming situation considering that the US debt, in 1988, was only half of America's economic output.)

So at some point in time, as the federal debt continues to rise, the world's desire to invest in US assets, including the debt, will diminish, interest rates will very quickly skyrocket, and the value of the dollar will plummet, causing another great economic recession or even a depression. If America were to lose its status of providing the world's primary currency for international commerce, it will be catastrophic. In fact, recognizing how disastrous this would be for the US economy, in recent years, rival nations, like Iran, Russia, and North Korea, have attempted to undermine the US by trying to convince the rest of the world to switch over to another "more stable" international currency. So while the entire world is now watching, only the United States with its actions can either prevail or fall victim to their nefarious plans.

Of course, America's inability to reduce and ultimately pay off its debt can generate additional complications domestically as well. If local investors begin to doubt the government's ability to pay its dues, they could either dispose of their US assets, thus escalating the crisis, or demand much higher rates for their investment, thus driving interest rates even higher, making it harder for business and individuals to borrow money. Over time, low confidence and reduced investments will slow down productivity, and as a result, the wages of American workers will decline.

Due to the rising debt, the Congressional Budget Office (CBO) estimates that in the next twenty years, the annual income of a family of four (when adjusted for inflation) will be worth $16,000 less than today! A disturbing estimate not only for the 44 percent of people whose earnings today can buy less than the minimum wage in 1968, but to every American, since within the next two decades, with the value of the dollar going down and the cost of living going up, millions more will be joining those already struggling to make ends meet. Less disposable income will make it harder for families to buy houses and cars, pay for college education, or buy other products and services.

Slow economic growth will not only affect the lives of working Americans but will also make America's fiscal challenges worse. Reduced personal income means a reduction in federal tax revenue, which puts the federal budget even further out of balance. Gradually, money for vital social programs (including those for senior citizens and veterans), not to mention investment capital desperately needed for America's crumbling infrastructure (highways, bridges, utility grids), will all but disappear.

The CBO further predicts that in the next ten years the US will pay $5.2 trillion to cover the interest on the national debt alone. It also estimates that by 2047, servicing the interest on the national debt will be the second largest government program, and only two years later, by 2049, it will become the single most expensive program. Yet, this will not be an investment toward America's future, but a harsh penalty for current mistakes.

SUPPORT THE FOLLOWING/ HELP REDUCE THE NATIONAL DEBT	ANNUAL SAVINGS
Raise the minimum wage, save on welfare benefits.(³)	$300 billion
Reduce military budget to levels prior to the Iraq War.	$350 billion
Eliminate subsidies to established corporations.	$100 billion
Abolish Medicare Part D and negotiate drug prices.	$7 billion
Eliminate hedge fund managers' loopholes.	$83 billion
Adjust the federal mortgage deduction loophole.	$70 billion
Abolish tax credits to big oil and gas companies.	$5 billion
No longer allow fines to be used as tax deductions.	$20 billion
Lower corporate tax rate, eliminate other loopholes.(⁴)	$200 billion
Insist corporations pay taxes for their overseas profits.	$40 billion
Eliminate loopholes that allow shifting profits overseas.	$100 billion
Decriminalize and highly regulate illegal "soft" drugs.(⁵)	$102 billion
POTENTIAL SAVINGS	**$1.37 trillion**

---

3 *A minimum wage of $15/hour not only will help reduce the number of those relying on welfare by as much as 50 percent, which in turn will save the taxpayer $300 billion each year in social benefits but will further stimulate the economy with an additional disposable income of $100 billion annually. This money, in the hands of lower-income Americans, will be used for everyday necessities. Not only will it buy more products and services (gas, groceries, fast food, clothing), but it will also help produce additional tax revenue at both the local and federal levels. Moreover, an added disposable income of $100 billion into the economy every year, will certainly increase the revenue of many businesses and help offset the higher cost of the minimum wage.*

4 *Enticing US corporations to repatriate their existing overseas profits by reducing the corporate tax to a 12–15% rate could help generate an additional one-time tax revenue of $500 billion. (Currently, several American Companies, hold $2.6 trillion in tax haven countries to avoid paying taxes in the US.)*

5 *In 2016, Colorado collected $150 million in excise taxes from legal marijuana sales (it's worth noting that the first $40 million Colorado receives each year go to fund school projects). ArcView group (a cannabis industry research firm) estimates that the legal marijuana industry in the US could reach $22 billion in annual sales by 2020. The eight states where currently the use of recreational marijuana is legal (Maine, Massachusetts, Colorado, California, Nevada, Oregon, Washington, Alaska) at the average excise tax rate of 15 percent, they tend to make $3 billion in taxes each year collectively. Legalizing the use of recreational marijuana over the entire US could conservatively generate an additional tax revenue of $20 billion (not to mention the savings from decreased incarceration and law enforcement.) In the current environment where consumers do not want higher income taxes or sales taxes, this additional excise tax revenue (as in the case of alcohol and tobacco) can be used to fund education, infrastructure work, and social programs.*

The smart people who are too smart to vote, they are governed by the decisions of the idiots who do.

— Plato, 380 BC

Bibliography

"17 Numbers That Will Make You Realize Just How Pathetic the Minimum Wage Is." (2014, September 24). Retrieved from www. huffingtonpost.com/2014/09/24/minimum-wage-increase.

"2014 AHAR: Part 1 – PIT Estimates of Homelessness in the US." (n.d.). Retrieved from https://www.hudexchange.info/ resource/4074/2014-ahar-part-1-pit-estimates-of-homelessness/.

"2015 Small Area Income and Poverty Estimates." (2016, December 14). Retrieved from https://www.census.gov/ newsroom/press-releases/2016/cb16-tps153.html.

"7 Corporate Giants Accused of Evading Billions in Taxes." Retrieved from http://fortune. com/2016/03/11/apple-google-taxes-eu/

About CRS. (n.d.). Retrieved from https:// www.loc.gov/crsinfo/about/.

Aguadito. (2013, February 15). "Thoughts on the Minimum Wage: Evidence, Opposition, and Historical

Context." Retrieved from http://www.dailykos.com/
story/2013/2/14/1187280/-Thoughts-on-the-Minimum-Wage.

Alexander, D. (2015, October 06). "Big US Firms Hold
$2.1 Trillion Overseas to Avoid Taxes: Study." (E. Beech,
Ed.). Retrieved from http://www.reuters.com/article/
us-usa-tax-offshore-idUSKCN0S008U20151006.

"American Dream." (n.d.). Retrieved from https://
en.wikipedia.org/wiki/American_Dream.

Amadeo, K. (n.d.). "Does the Government Lie About
Unemployment?" Retrieved from https://www.thebal-
ance.com/what-is-the-real-unemployment-rate-3306198.

"America's Middle Class Is Shrinking." (2015, June).
Retrieved from https://www.whitehutchinson.com/
news/lenews/2015/june/article105.shtml.

"An Analysis of Where American Companies Report
Profits: Indications of Profit Shifting." Retrieved from
https://fas.org/sgp/crs/misc/R42927.pdf.

"Annual Survey of State Government Tax Collections."
(2017, April 18). Retrieved from https://www.cen-
sus.gov/newsroom/press-releases/2017/cb17-
tps37-state-government-tax-collections.html.

Becker, S. (2015, June 12). "How Much Do Welfare Programs
Cost the US? More than You Ever Thought." Retrieved from
http://www.cheatsheet.com/business/why-is-american-so-
cial-welfare-so-incredibly-expensive.html/?a=viewall.

Bureau of Economic Analysis. (n.d.). Retrieved
from https://www.bea.gov/.

"Brainwashing: 6 Methods and Ways to Avoid It."
(2007, December 13). Retrieved from http://news.
softpedia.com/news/Brainwashing-6-Methods-
and-5-Ways-to-Avoid-it-73804.shtml.

Chameides, B. (2014, May 02). "Following the Money: Energy
Dollars Hard at Work on Capitol Hill." Retrieved from http://
energyblog.nationalgeographic.com/2014/05/02/following-
the-money-energy-dollars-hard-at-work-on-capitol-hill/.

Chantrill, C. (2017, April 23). "What Is the Spending
on Welfare?" Retrieved from http://www.usgovern-
mentspending.com/us_welfare_spending_40.html.

Chen, M. (June 29, 2015). "Is Walmart Hiding
$76 Billion in Overseas Tax Havens?" Retrieved
from https://www.thenation.com/article/
is-walmart-hiding-76-billion-in-overseas-tax-havens/.

Chokshi, N. (2015, March 18). "The United States of Subsidies:
The Biggest Corporate Winners in Each State." Retrieved
from https://www.washingtonpost.com/blogs/govbeat/
wp/2015/03/17/the-united-states-of-subsidies-the-biggest-
corporate-winners-in-each-state/?utm_term=.adb380787ca0.

Chokshi, N. (2016, April 04). "Calif. and NY Are Getting a $15
Minimum Wage. Here's How Much That Buys Everywhere
Else." Retrieved from https://www.washingtonpost.
com/news/wonk/wp/2016/04/04/california-and-new-
york-are-getting-a-15-minimum-wage-heres-how-much-
that-buys-everywhere-else/?utm_term=.e2e2ce329b84.

Christoforou, C. (2016, February 15). "Deloitte Cyprus
Tax Facts 2016." Retrieved from https://www2.
deloitte.com/content/dam/Deloitte/cy/Documents/
tax/CY_Tax_TaxFacts2016EN_Noexp.pdf.

Clausing, K. (2016, March 25). "The Effect of Profit Shifting on the Corporate Tax Base." Retrieved from http://www.taxanalysts.org/content/effect-profit-shifting-corporate-tax-base

Clemente, F. (2015, June 24). "The Walmart Web: How the World's Biggest Corporation Secretly Uses Tax Havens to Dodge Taxes." Retrieved from https://americansfortaxfairness.org/the-walmart-web/.

Cohn, E. (2014, July 10). "New Analysis Debunks Claim That a Higher Minimum Wage Kills Job Growth." Retrieved from http://www.huffingtonpost.com/2014/07/10/minimum-wage-kill-jobs_n_5571412.html.

"College Enrollment and Work Activity of 2015 High School Graduates." (2016, April 28). Retrieved from https://www.bls.gov/news.release/hsgec.nr0.htm.

Colson, T. (2016, December 29). "A Future between Star Trek and the Matrix: Automation Could Destroy 15 Million UK Jobs in the Next Two Decades." Retrieved from http://www.businessinsider.com/ippr-automation-robots-could-destroy-15-million-uk-jobs-in-next-two-decades-2016-12.

"Confronting the Unsustainable Growth of Welfare Entitlements: Principles of Reform and the Next Steps." (2010, June 24). Retrieved, from http://www.heritage.org/welfare/report/confronting-the-unsustainable-growth-welfare-entitlements-principles-reform.

Connerly, W., PhD. (2005, March 29). "Unemployment Insurance in a Free Society." Retrieved from http://www.ncpa.org/pub/st274?pg=3.

"Corporatism." (n.d.). Retrieved from https://en.wikipedia.org/wiki/Corporatism.

"Cost of Living in Seattle." (n.d.). Retrieved from https://www.numbeo.com/cost-of-living/in/Seattle.

"Current Population Survey (CPS)." (2017, April 23). Retrieved from https://www.bls.gov/cps/.

"Cyprus Not an Offshore Tax Haven." (n.d.). Retrieved from http://www.investment-gateway.eu/credible_jurisdiction.asp.

Delaney, A., and Scheller, A. (2015, February 28). "Who Gets Food Stamps? White People, Mostly." Retrieved from http://www.huffingtonpost.com/2015/02/28/food-stamp-demographics_n_6771938.html.

Denavas-Walt, C., and Proctor, D. (2014). "Income and Poverty in the United States: 2013." Retrieved August 06, 2017 from https://www.census.gov/content/dam/Census/library/publications/2014/demo/p60-249.pdf.

"Democratic Capitalism." (n.d.). Retrieved from https://en.wikipedia.org/wiki/Democratic_capitalism.

Drucker, J., and Dudley, R. (2015, June 17). "Wal-Mart Has $76 Billion in Undisclosed Overseas Tax Havens." Retrieved from https://www.bloomberg.com/news/articles/2015-06-17/wal-mart-has-76-billion-in-overseas-tax-havens-report-says.

"Econ and Things: On the Three Kinds of Lies." (n.d.). Retrieved from https://josethebae.wordpress.com/.

"Eisenhower Warns of Military-Industrial Complex." (n.d.). Retrieved from http://www.history.com/this-day-in-history/eisenhower-warns-of-military-industrial-complex.

"Eisenhower Warns Us of the Military Industrial Complex." (2006, August 04). Retrieved from https://www.youtube.com/watch?v=8y06NSBBRtY.

Etehad, M., and Lin, J. C. (2016, August 13). "The World Is Getting Better at Paid Maternity Leave. The US Is Not." Retrieved from https://www.washingtonpost.com/news/worldviews/wp/2016/08/13/the-world-is-getting-better-at-paid-maternity-leave-the-u-s-is-not/?utm_term=.b2e918574a26.

"Energy subsidies." (2017, April 11). Retrieved from https://en.wikipedia.org/wiki/Energy_subsidies.

"European Central Bank—Statistics Paper Series, No. 2/April 2013. The Eurosystem Household Finance and Consumption Survey Results from the First Wave." Retrieved from http://www.ecb.europa.eu/pub/pdf/other/ecbsp2en.pdf?0696a13c1992dcabc79eebed533574f2.

Eyermann, C. (2015, March 24). "Who Owns the 'Public' Portion of the National Debt?" Retrieved from http://www.mygovcost.org/2015/03/24/who-owns-the-public-portion-of-the-national-debt/.

Fairchild, C. (2013, September 18). "Middle-Class Decline Mirrors the Fall of Unions in One Chart." Retrieved from http://www.huffingtonpost.com/2013/09/18/union-membership-middle-class-income_n_3948543.html.

"Federal Reserve Board Announces Termination of Enforcement Action." (2017, April 11). Retrieved from https://www.federalreserve.gov/.

"Federal Revenue: Where Does the Money Come From?" (n.d.). Retrieved from https://www.nationalpriorities.org/budget-basics/federal-budget-101/revenues/.

"Fees Extra Costs When Buying property in Cyprus."
Retrieved from https://www.justlanded.com/
english/Cyprus/Cyprus-Guide/Property/Fees.

"Global Wealth Report 2016 by Credit Suisse." Retrieved from
http://publications.credit-suisse.com/tasks/render/file/
index.cfm?fileid=AD783798-ED07-E8C2-4405996B5B02A32E.

Gongloff, M. (2013, May 22). "The 1 Chart That Reveals
Just How Grossly Unfair The US Tax System Has Become."
Retrieved from http://www.huffingtonpost.com/2013/05/22/
chart-shows-corp-taxes-grossly-unfair_n_3321737.html.

"Governor Cuomo Signs $15 Minimum Wage Plan and
12 Week Paid Family Leave Policy into Law." (2016, May
06). Retrieved from https://www.governor.ny.gov/
news/governor-cuomo-signs-15-minimum-wage-
plan-and-12-week-paid-family-leave-policy-law.

Grajales, C. (2014, March 4). "The Statistics of
Drug Legalization." Retrieved from http://www.
statisticsviews.com/details/feature/5914551/
The-statistics-of-drug-legalization.html.

Greenebaum, H. (2015, December 06). "Why Is US Minimum
Wage Less than Half What Australia Pays Their Workers?"
Retrieved from http://www.ibtimes.com/why-us-minimum-
wage-less-half-what-australia-pays-their-workers-722579.

Haislmaier, E., and Gonshorowski, D. (2017, April 26).
"Freeing States from the Obamacare Insurance Mandates."
Retrieved from http://www.heritage.org/health-care-reform/
report/freeing-states-the-obamacare-insurance-mandates.

"Health and Social Care Spending as a Percentage of GDP."
(n.d.). Retrieved from http://www.commonwealthfund.org/

interactives-and-data/chart-cart/issue-brief/us-health-care-global-perspectives-oecd/health-and-social-care-spending-as-a-percentage-of-gdp.

"'How Propaganda Works' Is a Timely Reminder for a Post-Truth Age." (2016, December 26) *New York Times*. Retrieved from https://www.nytimes.com/2016/12/26/books/how-propaganda-works-is-a-timely-reminder-for-a-post-truth-age.html?mcubz=0.

"The Heritage Foundation: The Many Real Dangers of Soaring National Debt." (2013, June 18). Retrieved from http://www.heritage.org/budget-and-spending/report/the-many-real-dangers-soaring-national-debt.

"Hours of Work in US History." (n.d.). Retrieved, from https://eh.net/encyclopedia/hours-of-work-in-u-s-history/.

"How Many Americans Earn More Than $100,000?" (n.d.). Retrieved from https://www.reference.com/business-finance/many-americans-earn-100-000-d9640c33803c84d2.

"How Walmart Hiding $76 Billion in Secret Subsidiaries around the World." Retrieved from https://www.dailykos.com/stories/2015/6/17/1393999/-How-Walmart-s-hiding-76-billion-in-secret-subsidiaries-around-the-world.

"Interest Expense on US Debt." (n.d.). Retrieved from https://www.treasurydirect.gov/govt/reports/ir/ir_expense.htm.

Jarro, M. (n.d.). "Fortune 500 Companies and Tax Havens: A Study." Retrieved from https://taxlinked.net/blog/october-2016/fortune-500-companies-tax-havens-a-study.

Jeffrey, T. (2014, October 03). "The 35.4 Percent: 109,631,000 on Welfare." Retrieved from http://www.cnsnews.com/commentary/terence-p-jeffrey/354-percent-109631000-welfare.

Konczal, M., and Covert, B. (2014, October 27). "The Score: Does the Minimum Wage Kill Jobs?" Retrieved from https://www.thenation.com/article/score-does-minimum-wage-kill-jobs/.

"Labor Movement." (n.d.). Retrieved from http://www.history.com/topics/labor.

Lamothe, D. (2015, February 02). "How Obama's New Defense Budget Looks like Reagan's." Retrieved from https://www.washingtonpost.com/news/checkpoint/wp/2015/02/02/how-obamas-new-defense-budget-looks-like-reagans/?utm_term=.e545d77779ae.

Lauter, D. (2016, August 14). "How Do Americans View Poverty? Many Blue-Collar Whites, Key to Trump, Criticize Poor People as Lazy and Content to Stay on Welfare." Retrieved from http://www.latimes.com/projects/la-na-pol-poverty-poll/.

Lawson, J. (2016, January 16). "How Inflation Affects Your Cost of Living." Retrieved from http://jameslawson.ws/how-inflation-affects-your-cost-of-living/.

Leonhardt, D. (2016, December 08). "Opinion: The American Dream, Quantified at Last." Retrieved from https://www.nytimes.com/2016/12/08/opinion/the-american-dream-quantified-at-last.html?_r=0.

Livingston, G. (2016, September 26). "Among 41 Nations, US Is the Outlier When It Comes to Paid Parental Leave." Retrieved from http://www.pewresearch.org/fact-tank/2016/09/26/u-s-lacks-mandated-paid-parental-leave/.

McCain, J. (2013, May 21). "Shifting Profits Offshore to Avoid US Taxes." Retrieved from https://www.c-span.org/video/?c4452620%2Fshifting-profits-offshore-avoid-us-taxes.

McCane, L. (2016, March 18). "Kentucky House Approves House Bill 626, Bill Would Allow Students to Attend Community College for Free." Retrieved from http://www.inquisitr.com/2902309/kentucky-house-approves-house-bill-626-bill-would-allow-students-to-attend-community-college-for-free/.

McIntyre, R. (2017, March 06). "News Release: ITEP and CTJ Boards Announce Alan Essig as New Executive Director." Retrieved from http://ctj.org/ctjreports/#.WP0kWaITUjF.

McKay, T. (2015, October 25). "6 Charts Show How Ridiculous US Drug Prices Are, Compared to Other Countries." Retrieved from https://mic.com/articles/125688/here-s-how-much-more-the-us-spends-on-medicine-than-everyone-else-in-6-charts#.z55kmlKpW.

"Medical Tourism." (n.d.). Retrieved from http://medicaltourism.com/(X(1)S(eb2lbcsuejfeiuvkpqklfjyr))/Forms/Jordan/keysectors.aspx.

"Media's Use of Propaganda to Persuade People's Attitude, Beliefs and Behaviors." Retrieved from https://web.stanford.edu/class/e297c/war_peace/media/hpropaganda.html.

Matthews, D. (2012, August 28). "Defense Spending in the US, in Four Charts." Retrieved from https://www.washingtonpost.com/news/wonk/wp/2012/08/28/defense-spending-in-the-u-s-in-four-charts/?utm_term=.bc02f6310763.

Matthews, D. (2013, August 19). "The US has a $7.25 minimum wage. Australia's is $16.88." Retrieved from

https://www.washingtonpost.com/news/wonk/
wp/2013/08/19/the-u-s-has-a-7-25-minimum-wage-
australias-is-16-88/?utm_term=.0b0563a34501.

Merle, R. (2016, May 10). "US Companies Are Saving
$100 Billion a Year by Shifting Profits Overseas, Report
Says." Retrieved from https://www.washingtonpost.
com/news/business/wp/2016/05/10/u-s-compa-
nies-are-saving-100-billion-a-year-by-shifting-profits-
overseas-report-says/?utm_term=.be03c96d8f39.

"Military Budget of the United States." (2017, April
24). Retrieved from https://en.wikipedia.org/
wiki/Military_budget_of_the_United_States.

Miller, G. (2017, February 2). "The US is the Most Overworked
Developed Nation in the World: When Do We Draw the
Line?" Retrieved from https://20somethingfinance.com/
american-hours-worked-productivity-vacation/.

Mirhaydari, A. (2016, August 01). "The Only Reason the US
Economy Isn't Crashing." Retrieved from http://www.cbsnews.
com/news/the-only-reason-the-u-s-economy-isnt-crashing/.

Millan, L. (n.d.). "Ambitious International Effort to Rewrite
Tax Rules at Risk." Retrieved from http://lawinquebec.com/
ambitious-international-effort-to-rewrite-tax-rules-at-risk/.

Nittoloi, J. (2016, August 10). "An Innovative Solution to
Income Inequality." Retrieved from https://tcf.org/content/
about-tcf/an-innovative-solution-to-income-inequality/.

Norris, F. (2014, April 25). "Fewer US Graduates Opt
for College after High School." Retrieved from https://
www.nytimes.com/2014/04/26/business/fewer-us-
high-school-graduates-opt-for-college.html?_r=0.

Nielsen, N. (n.d.) ECB: "German Households Less Wealthy than Cypriots." Retrieved August 04, 2017, from https://euobserver.com/economics/119751.

Oak, R. (2014, December 28). "China Trade Deficit Has Cost the United States 3.2 Million Jobs." Retrieved from http://www.economicpopulist.org/content/china-trade-deficit-has-cost-united-states-32-million-jobs-5645.

Oakford, S. (2016, April 19). "Portugal's Example: What Happened after It Decriminalized All Drugs, from Weed to Heroin." Retrieved from https://news.vice.com/article/ungass-portugal-what-happened-after-decriminalization-drugs-weed-to-heroin.

"Offshore Shell Games 2016: The Use of Offshore Tax Havens by Fortune 500 Companies." Retrieved from http://ctj.org/pdf/offshoreshellgames2016.pdf.

"Office of Management and Budget." (2017, April 10). Retrieved from https://www.whitehouse.gov/omb.

"Offshore Shell Games: The Use of Offshore Tax Heavens by the Top 100 Publicly Traded Companies." Retrieved from http://www.uspirg.org/sites/pirg/files/reports/Offshore_Shell_Games_USPIRG.pdf.

Peralta, K. (2014, December 11). "Outsourcing to China Cost US 3.2 Million Jobs Since 2001." Retrieved from https://www.usnews.com/news/blogs/data-mine/2014/12/11/outsourcing-to-china-cost-us-32-million-jobs-since-2001.

Peart, D. (n.d.). "The Almighty Dollar: 2016 and the Long History of Lobbying." Common-place: The Journal of early American Life. Retrieved from http://common-place.org/book/2016-will-mark-not-just-the-election-of-the-forty-fifth-president-of-the-united-states-but-also-the-200th-anniversary-of-the-creation-of-the-first-ever-lobbying-agency-in-the-national-capital/.

Perry, M. (2015, October 1). "Today Is Manufacturing Day, So Let's Recognize America's World-Class Manufacturing Sector and Factory Workers AEI." Retrieved from https://www.aei.org/publication/october-2-is-manufacturing-day-so-lets-recognize-americas-world-class-manufacturing-sector-and-factory-workers/.

Perry, M. J. (2017, April 23). "Sunday Afternoon Links." Retrieved from https://www.aei.org/publication/blog/carpe-diem/.

Peter G. Peterson. "Foundation: The Fiscal and Economic Impact." Retrieved from http://www.pgpf.org/the-fiscal-and-economic-challenge/fiscal-and-economic-impact.

Pettinger, T. (n.d.). "Pros and Cons of Capitalism." Retrieved from http://www.economicshelp.org/blog/5002/economics/pros-and-cons-of-capitalism/.

Phillips, R., Gardner, M., Kitson, K., Robins, A., and Surka, M. (2016, October 04). "Offshore Shell Games 2016." Retrieved from http://ctj.org/ctjreports/2016/10/offshore_shell_games_2016.php#.WQJf7aITUjE.

Plumer, B. (2013, January 07). "America's Staggering Defense Budget in Charts." Retrieved from https://www.washingtonpost.com/news/wonk/wp/2013/01/07/everything-chuck-hagel-needs-to-know-about-the-defense-budget-in-charts/.

Piketty, T., Saez, E., and Zucman, G. (2017, April 05). "Economic Growth in the United States: A Tale of Two Countries." Retrieved August 04, 2017, from

http://equitablegrowth.org/research-analysis/
economic-growth-in-the-united-states-a-tale-of-two-countries/.

Potter, W. (2015, January 26). "Health Insurers Watch Profits
Soar as They Dump Small Business Customers." Retrieved from
https://www.publicintegrity.org/2015/01/26/16658/health-in-
surers-watch-profits-soar-they-dump-small-business-customers.

Proctor, B., Senegal, J., and Killar, M. (2016). "Income and
Poverty in the United States: 2015." Retrieved August
06, 2017 from https://www.census.gov/content/dam/
Census/library/publications/2016/demo/p60-256.pdf.

"Profit Shifting." Retrieved from https://www.
bloomberg.com/quicktake/profit-shifting.

Quigley, A. (2016, July 27). "Seattle's Increased
Minimum Wage Has Had Little Effect So Far."
Retrieved from http://www.businessinsider.com/
seattle-increased-minimum-wage-effects-2016-7.

Quigley, B. (2014, January 14). "Ten Examples of Welfare
for the Rich and Corporations." Retrieved from http://
www.huffingtonpost.com/bill-quigley/ten-examples-of-
welfare-for-the-rich-and-corporations_b_4589188.html.

Ramshield, D. (2010, December 05). "Death of the
American Dream." Retrieved from http://www.
dailykos.com/story/2010/12/5/925448/.

"Real Minimum Wages." (n.d.). Retrieved from https://
stats.oecd.org/Index.aspx?DataSetCode=RMW.

Reed, R. (2016, June 06). "Watch John Oliver Forgive $15 Million
in Debt." Retrieved from http://www.rollingstone.com/tv/
news/watch-john-oliver-forgive-15-million-in-debt-20160606.

"Research and Ideas for Shared Prosperity." (n.d.). Retrieved from http://www.epi.org/.

Reich, R. (2015, March 09). "Robert Reich: How Big Corporations Are Systematically Screwing Us Over." Retrieved from http://www.alternet.org/economy/robert-reich-how-big-corporations-are-systematically-screwing-us-over.

"Rigged Reform: US Companies Are Dodging Billions in Taxes." (n.d.). Retrieved from https://www.oxfamamerica.org/explore/research-publications/rigged-reform/.

Rojo, J. (2013, April 15). "Corporate Tax Dodgers: 10 Companies and Their Tax Loopholes." Retrieved from http://www.ips-dc.org/corporate_tax_dodgers/.

Rotman, D. (2013, June 01). "How Technology Is Destroying Jobs." Retrieved from https://www.technologyreview.com/s/515926/how-technology-is-destroying-jobs/.

Rotman, D. (2016, September 01). "Will Advances in Technology Create a Jobless Future?" Retrieved from https://www.technologyreview.com/s/538401/who-will-own-the-robots/.

Rugy, V. (2016, September 14). "Thirty-Two Years of Bipartisan Debt-Ceiling Raises." Retrieved from https://www.mercatus.org/publication/thirty-two-years-bipartisan-debt-ceiling-raises.

Sandelius, S. (2013). "Rept: ECB Data: Cypriots on Average 3-Times Richer than Germans." Retrieved August 06, 2017 from https://www.marketnews.com/content/rpt-ecb-data-cypriots-average-3-times-richer-germans.

Savage, C. (2015, December 21). "38 Pictures That Show the Decline of America since the 1950s." Retrieved from http://www.returnofkings.com/75440/38-pictures-that-show-the-decline-of-america-since-the-1950s

"Secretary of the Treasury Steven T. Mnuchin." (n.d.). Retrieved from https://www.treasury.gov/Pages/default.aspx.

Schoen, J. W. (2015, October 06). "US Companies Hold $2.1 Trillion Offshore." Retrieved from http://www.cnbc.com/2015/10/06/us-companies-holding-21-trillion-offshore-profits.html.

"Seven Decisive Pros and Cons of Capitalism." (n.d.). Retrieved from https://greengarageblog.org/7-decisive-pros-and-cons-of-capitalism.

"Seven Myths about Weed." (2017, March 8). Retrieved from http://howtorollthebestjointin-theworld.com/7-myths-about-weed/.

Shaw, J. (2015, June 17). "Ten Statistics You Didn't Know about Veteran Homelessness." Retrieved from http://www.newsmax.com/FastFeatures/homeless-veterans-statistics/2015/06/17/id/651049/.

"Sheltering Foreign Profits from US Taxes Is No Big Feat." Retrieved from https://www.wsj.com/articles/sheltering-foreign-profits-from-u-s-taxes-is-no-big-feat-1461627831.

Shedlock, M. (2012, July 7). "What Role Does Government Play in Price Inflation?" Retrieved from http://www.financialsense.com/contributors/michael-shedlock/what-role-does-government-play-in-price-inflation.

"Show Us The Local Subsidies." (n.d.). Retrieved from http://www.goodjobsfirst.org/.

Shenker-Osorio, A. (2013, August 01). "Why Americans All Believe They Are 'Middle Class.'" Retrieved from https://www.theatlantic.com/politics/archive/2013/08/why-americans-all-believe-they-are-middle-class/278240/.

Simon, K. (1972, November 30). "Digest of Educational Statistics, 1972 Edition." Retrieved from https://eric.ed.gov/?id=ED083677.

Sinn, M. (2016, November 04). "NEWS FLASH: US Government Wastes $1.5 Trillion on Devastating Drug War." Retrieved from https://thinkbynumbers.org/government-spending/drug-war-statistics/.

"Social program Cost by Country." (n.d.). Retrieved from https://www.google.com/search?q=social%2B-program%2Bcost%2Bby%2Bcountryandrlz=1C1CHWA_enUS615US616andespv=2andbiw=1286andbi-h=864andsource=lnmsandtbm=ischandsa=Xand-ved=0ahUKEwiai8n9_Z3OAhUEQSYKHVg0BNUQ_AUIBigB#imgrc=MvF_kfC8t24LsM%3A.

"Social market economy." (n.d.). Retrieved from http://www.thefreedictionary.com/Social market economy.

Spielberg, B., and Bernstein, J. (2015, November 17). "The Truth about the Minimum Wage." Retrieved from http://www.msnbc.com/msnbc/the-truth-about-the-minimum-wage.

Squires, D., and Anderson, C. (2015, October 01). US Healthcare from a Global Perspective: Spending, Use of Services, Pricing, and Health in 13 Countries. Retrieved, from http://www.commonwealthfund.org/publi-cations/view-all-reports-and-briefs#/q=global%20perspectiveandsort=%40fdate63677%20descending.

"Study Finds US Companies Shifting Profits Overseas." Retrieved from *New York Times* http://www.nytimes.com/2004/09/13/business/worldbusiness/study-finds-us-companies-shifting-profits-overseas.html?mcubz=0.

Story, L. (2012, January 12). "As Companies Seek Tax Deals, Governments Pay High Price." Retrieved from http://www.nytimes.com/2012/12/02/us/how-local-taxpayers-bankroll-corporations.html?_r=2and.

Surowiecki, J. (2014, September 14). "Give the Homeless Homes." Retrieved from http://www.newyorker.com/magazine/2014/09/22/home-free.

"Tax Haven: Cyprus." (n.d.). Retrieved from http://www.taxhavens.biz/european_tax_havens/tax_haven_cyprus/.

"Tax, Facts and Figures 2017—Cyprus." (2017, January 01). Retrieved from http://www.pwc.com.cy/en/publications-newsletters/tax-facts-figures-2017.html.

"The State of Homelessness in America 2016." (2016, April 06). Retrieved from http://www.endhomelessness.org/library/entry/SOH2016.

"*The Telegraph*: America's Reckless Money-Printing Could Put the World Back into Crisis, April 30, 2011." Retrieved from http://www.telegraph.co.uk/finance/comment/liamhalligan/8484530/Americas-reckless-money-printing-could-put-the-world-back-into-crisis.html.

"The Walmart Web: How the World's Biggest Corporation Secretly Uses Tax Havens to Dodge Taxes." Retrieved from https://americansfortaxfairness.org/files/TheWalmartWeb-June-2015-FINAL.pdf.

Thompson, M. (2015, January 01). "The True Cost of the Afghanistan War May Surprise You." Retrieved from http://time.com/3651697/afghanistan-war-cost/.

"Three Oil and Gas Tax Loopholes and Subsidies You Didn't Know About." (2016, December 27). Retrieved from https://www.green-buildings.com/articles/3-oil-and-gas-tax-loopholes-and-subsidies-you-didnt-know-about/.

Timeline of United States at war. (n.d.). Retrieved from https://en.wikipedia.org/wiki/Timeline_of_United_States_at_war

"Top 10 Corporate Tax Avoiders." Retrieved from https://www.sanders.senate.gov/top-10-corporate-tax-avoiders.

Tokin, C. (2012, April 23). "Patients in the Dark on Medical Costs, Study Finds." Retrieved from http://abcnews.go.com/Health/medical-costs-vary-wildly-hospital-hospital-study/story?id=16196700.

"US Correctional Problems." (n.d.). Retrieved from https://www.justleadershipusa.org/about-us/.

"US Companies Are Saving $100 Billion a Year by Shifting Profits Overseas, Report Say." Retrieved from the *Washington Post* https://www.washingtonpost.com/news/business/wp/2016/05/10/u-s-compa-nies-are-saving-100-billion-a-year-by-shifting-profits-overseas-report-says/?utm_term=.fb8ced6f36ba.

"US Corporations Have $1.4TN Hidden in Tax Havens, Larger than the Combined Economic Output of Russia, South Korea and Spain, Claims OXFAM Report" (2016, April 18). Retrieved from http://www.awdnews.com/economy/us-corporations-have-$1-4tn-hidden-in-tax-havens,-larger-than-the-combined-economic-output-of-russia,-south-korea-and-spain,-claims-oxfam-report.

"US Economic Indicators." (n.d.). Retrieved from http://www.tradingeconomics.com/united-states/indicators.

"US Household Income." (n.d.). Retrieved from http://www.deptofnumbers.com/income/us/.

"US military Budget by President." (n.d.). Retrieved from https://www.google.com/search?q=us%2Bmilitary%2Bbudget%2Bby%2Bpresidentandrlz=1C1CHWA_enUS615US616andespv=2andbiw=1327andbih=864andsource=lnmsandtbm=ischandsa=Xandved=0ahUKEwiriPzo8oDOAhVCOCYKHajWA10Q_AUIBygC#tbm=ischandq=us defense spending by presidentandimgrc=_.

"United States: How's Life?" (n.d.). Retrieved from http://www.oecdbetterlifeindex.org/countries/united-states/

"United States Average Hourly Wages 1964–2017." (n.d.). Retrieved from http://www.tradingeconomics.com/united-states/wages.

"United States Federal Minimum Hourly Wage 1938–2017." (n.d.). Retrieved from http://www.tradingeconomics.com/united-states/minimum-wages.

Wallace, C. (2017, February 06). "Government Receives Low Marks in Trust but High Marks in Performance: How It Can Influence Future Endeavors." Retrieved from http://patimes.org/government-receives-marks-trust-high-marks-performance-influence-future-endeavors/.

"Wall Street Journal: Corporations Save Billions as Americans Die Younger." Retrieved August 09, 2017

from http://www.msn.com/en-us/money/companies/
corporations-save-billions-as-americans-die-younger/
ar-AApHxE9?li=BBmkt5Randocid=spartandhp.

"Walmart Offshore Empire Exposed: Report Finds Retailer
Avoiding Billions in Taxes by Using International Tax
Havens." Retrieved from http://www.ibtimes.com/
walmarts-offshore-empire-exposed-report-finds-re-
tailer-avoiding-billions-taxes-using-1971129.

Walter, K., and Madland, D. (2011, January 20). "Report:
As Union Membership Rates Decrease, Middle Class
Incomes Shrink." Retrieved from https://think-
progress.org/report-as-union-membership-rates-de-
crease-middle-class-incomes-shrink-5b10cd7f3f67.

"What's Happening to American Democracy?" (2016,
March 23). Retrieved from http://www.aljazeera.com/
programmes/peopleandpower/2016/03/happen-
ing-american-democracy-160323094609454.html.

White, J. R. (2013, May 01). "United States Government
Accountability Office Report to Congressional Requesters.
Corporate Income Tax: Effective Tax Rates Can Differ
Significantly from the Statutory Rate." Retrieved
from www.gao.gov/assets/660/654957.pdf.

Wicks-Lim, J. (2016, April 05). "CA and NY Workers to Earn
$15 Minimum Wage, Will US Economy Suffer?" Retrieved
from https://www.youtube.com/watch?v=1Zlq0Q64uZ8.

Williams, S. (2016, March 13). "One Chart Every Middle-
Class American Needs to See." Retrieved from https://
www.fool.com/investing/general/2016/03/13/1-chart-
every-middle-class-american-needs-to-see.aspx.

"World Cannabis Laws." (n.d.). Retrieved from https://commons.wikimedia.org/wiki/File:World-cannabis-laws.png.

Zaldivar, R. A. (2016, July 13). "$10,345 per person: US health Care Spending Reaches New Peak." Retrieved from http://www.pbs.org/newshour/rundown/new-peak-us-health-care-spending-10345-per-person/.

Zillman, C. (2015, April 13). "Who Makes Less than $15 Per Hour, in 3 Charts." Retrieved from http://fortune.com/2015/04/13/who-makes-15-per-hour/.

Chart and Graph Credits

Page 16: "Percentage of Children in Poverty."
Source: US Census Bureau.

Page 17: "Over 100 Million People in US Now Receiving Some Form of Federal Welfare." Source: US Census Survey of Income and Program Participation — Produced by Senate Budget Committee Republican Staff; Ranking Member Jeff Sessions.

Page 18: "Inflation Comparison: Percent Growth." Source: Advisor Perspectives.

Page 19: "Living in Poverty Areas." Source: US Census Bureau.

Page 20: "Paid Vacation and Paid Holidays, OECD Nations, in Working Days." Source: OECD.

Page 21: "Poverty Rates by Age: 1959 to 2015." Source: US Census Bureau.

Page 22: "More than One-Third of Young Adults Live at Home." Source: US Census Bureau.

Page 27: "US Real Manufacturing Output vs. Employment, 1947–2014." Sources: Bureau of Labor Statistics, Federal Reserve.

Page 28: "Median Income by Age and Gender, 1950-2010." Source: US Census Bureau.

Page 30: "Most New Jobs Will Be in Low Skill Work that Cannot Be Offshored or Mechanized, but Fewer Americans Want Them." Source: Bureau of Labor Statistics.

Page 32: "Poverty Thresholds for 2015 by Family Size and Number of Related Children under 18." Source: US Census Bureau.

Page 37: "A Different Way of Measuring Poverty." Source: US Census Bureau.

Page 48: "Percentage Change in Employment in States That Raised the Minimum Wage." Source: Bureau of Labor Statistics.

Page 49: "Who Works at Minimum Wage?" Source: Bureau of Labor Statistics.

Page 50: "Top 10 Counties by Employment Growth." Source: US Census Bureau.

Page 53: "Who Owns the Debt?" Source: US Treasury Department.

Page 57: "The US Spends More on Drugs." Source: OECD Health Statistics 2013.

Page 65: "Individual and Corporate Income Taxes as Percent of Total Federal Revenue (1934–2015)." Source: National Priorities Project. www.nationalpriorities.org.

Page 67: "Federal Tax Revenue 2015: $3.18 Trillion." Source: National Priorities Project, www.nationalpriorities.org.

Page 71: "Incarcerated Americans (1920–21013)." Source: Just Leadership USA, Inc.

Page 72: "World Map of Drug Legalization." Source: Wiki file.

Page 80: "Corporate Income Taxes Are a Declining Share of Total Federal Revenue — Percentage of Total Revenue from Corporate Income Tax." Source: Office of Management and Budget.

Page 82: "CPI: College Tuition vs. US Home Prices vs. CPI: All Items, 1978–2010." Source: Bureau of Labor Statistics, Census.

Page 87: "Percent of Fortune 500 Companies with 2015 Subsidiaries in 20 Top Tax Havens." Source: Citizens for Tax Justice.

Page 90: "Top 30 Companies with the Most Money Held Offshore." Source: Institute on Taxation and Economic Policy.

CPSIA information can be obtained
at www.ICGtesting.com
Printed in the USA
FSHW01n0908030518
47552FS